ACTING-IN

Practical Applications of Psychodramatic Methods

Howard A. Blatner, M.D.

Springer Publishing Company, Inc.

To David and Alisa, my children, who
demonstrate that spontaneity and
creativity grow along with the natural
unfolding of true innocence.

Copyright © 1973
SPRINGER PUBLISHING COMPANY, INC.
200 Park Avenue South, New York, New York 10003

ISBN Number: 0-8261-1400-8
Library of Congress Catalog Card Number: 73-80598

Printed in U.S.A.

CONTENTS

FOREWORD

In 1921, I created Psychodrama out of the earlier work I did with group psychotherapy, sociometry, and improvisatory theatre. Since then I have written numerous books and scores of articles on the subject. Dr. Blatner's book, *Acting-In,* will be a good adjunct to my writings. This is an excellent work on the subject.

I am especially pleased that Dr. Blatner notes the theological basis of the method of psychodrama.

I have always tried to show that my approach was meant as much more than a psychotherapeutic method—my ideas have emphasized that *creativity* and *spontaneity* affect the very roots of *vitality* and spiritual development, and thus affect our involvements in every sphere of our lives. Furthermore, I have always wanted to have people attend to the processes of health, as well as to the problems of illness thus I am glad Dr. Blatner has noted the applications of psychodrama in the home, school, and world of business.

When I first met Dr. Blatner in 1968, he was a resident in Psychiatry at Stanford University. At that time he showed me a collection of writings by others in the field of psychodrama, along with a few additions of his own—a syllabus he had assembled entitled "Practical Aspects of Psychodrama." I encouraged him to continue his interest in psychodrama and to do more of his own writing. Apparently, he has taken my advice.

I am further pleased with the different audiences to which this book can be addressed: for those who are interested in learning about psychodrama, it can be an introduction; for those who are practioners, these materials can comprise a useful handbook; and for the serious student, *Acting-In* is an up-to-date and extensive resource for references and background materials.

I wish the author every success in this undertaking.

J.L. MORENO, M.D.

PREFACE

The ancient Greeks used the drama as a ritual for the purpose of evoking a group catharsis. While the other artistic media have also served to express feelings and images, it was the drama that fully utilized the collective element in the service of objectifying the cross-currents of the soul and the dilemmas of the human condition. The drama in this sense had healing powers in that it clarified the unexpressed experiences and helped the individual to accept more fully the various facets of the personality.

The synthesis of the media of drama with the insights of modern psychology was chiefly developed by Dr. J.L. Moreno in his work with Psychodrama. The various applications of psychodramatic methods have been found to be effective in the fields of modern psychotherapy and education.

The major purpose of this book is to introduce the reader to the fundamental elements and basic principles related to the use of psychodramatic methods. Along with practical suggestions regarding technique, I include discussions of some of the theoretical bases of the use of the method. It is expected that the reader may need to modify these approaches to meet the requirements of his situation, and such creative adaptations are to be encouraged. To facilitate the reader's commitment to a serious study of the method, I also include extensive annotated references at the end of each chapter.

The reader may find many potential applications of the psychodramatic method such as: in fields of mental health, in group and individual psychotherapy, therapeutic community and drug abuse programs, occupational and activity therapy, etc.; in the fields of education , from the preschool level to the postgraduate professional training programs; in the churches, in pastoral counseling and group meetings; in business and industry, for organizational development, and leadership or personal relations training; encounter groups; and various other kinds of workshops.

In all of the above-mentioned fields, the use of action-oriented psychodramatic methods can complement traditional verbal approaches in order to facilitate the development of personal awareness and interpersonal sensitivity. It is the hope of the author that this book may help to increase the responsible applications of psychodramatic methods.

H. A. B.
PALO ALTO, CALIFORNIA
MAY, 1973

ACKNOWLEDGMENTS

I wish to thank the following people for sharing with me their ideas and materials: Marcia Karp Robbins, Adele Deeths McCormick, Barbara Seabourne, Eva Hitchcock Leveton, Hannah B. Weiner, Elaine Goldman, Carl Hollander, Betsy Drake Grant, Dr. Leon Fine, Dr. Anita Brothers, and, of course, Dr. and Mrs. J. L. Moreno. Finally, special thanks must go to my wife, Barbara, without whose encouragement and helpful criticism this book could never have been written.

Introduction

Many of the most powerful active approaches in contemporary psychotherapy and education are derived from the method of psychodrama, in which a person is helped to *enact* his problem instead of just *talking* about it. The purpose of this book is to introduce some practical applications of the psychodramatic method to readers from a variety of disciplines.

The psychodramatic method integrates the modes of cognitive analysis with the dimensions of *experiential* and *participatory involvement*. It not only partakes of the advantages of group therapy, but its uses of physical movement also bring the component of nonverbal cues to the attention of the participant. This is especially important not only for those who have little capacity for intellectual and verbal exploration (e.g., children, psychotics, delinquents, etc.), but also for those who tend to over-intellectualize their experiences. The most significant advantage of psychodrama, however, is that it converts the participant's urge toward "acting-out" into the constructive channel of "acting-in," which leads to insight.

"Acting-out" refers to the psychological defense mechanism by which the individual discharges his internal impulses through symbolic or actual enactment. Since the rationale for this defense mechanism occurs largely outside of consciousness, the individual experiences no sense of mastery or growth of self-understanding through his behavior. If the drive toward action could be channeled, the person might be able to make better use of his feelings. Through psychodramatic enactment, the impulses and their associated fantasies, memories, and projections are made consciously *explicit,* which serves to express these feelings while

1

simultaneously developing the individual's self-awareness.

In the use of the psychodramatic method, the tendency toward "acting-out" is encouraged, but within a structured group experience. What emerges is an enactment which turns the impulses into insights. Thus psychodrama facilitates not "acting-out," but what should be called "acting-in": the applications of *action* methods to the exploration of the psychological aspects of human experience.

In addition to the task of clarifying emotional conflicts, the psychodramatic method can be applied to the challenge of developing human potentialities. Through "acting-in," the individual can be reintroduced to many dimensions of personal experience that have been neglected in our contemporary, over-intellectualized society: creativity, spontaneity, drama, humor, playfulness, ritual, dance, body movement, physical contact, fantasy, music, nonverbal communication, and a widened role-repertoire. Western civilization has relegated many of these pursuits to childhood, the theater, or mythology, and in so doing, has drained our souls of their richest treasures. It is essential that we learn to recognize the vitality which can only grow within the context of play, and to cultivate and refine play so that we can preserve the spirit of childhood in our adult lives. Indeed, the task of integrating the experiential worlds of feelings, sensation, and imagination into our sterile existences may become a major goal of contemporary education and psychotherapy. In this book I will attempt to explicate in some detail how the psychodramatic method can reinforce this sense of play and experience.

PSYCHODRAMA AND PSYCHOTHERAPY: AN HISTORICAL COMPARISON

Psychodrama and psychoanalysis need not be at odds; rather, both are similar in that they act as *root* methods. Psychodrama, like psychoanalysis, can serve as a source of theory, technique and as a method of research. Furthermore, both approaches have been modified extensively and have been incorporated into other methods.

My own view is to liken psychodrama to the woodwind instruments of the orchestra: their introduction vastly extended and deepened the range of effects which were possible. This is because the mixture of two methods (or what Marshall McLuhan would call "media") results in the development of a totally new form which is more powerful and qualitatively different from the result of simple additive effects. So, too, does the addition of psychodramatic methods to conventional verbal forms extend the power of psychotherapy. Verbal and nonverbal forms need not be at opposite poles, for it is quite possible to interweave the aspects of cognitive and experiential, objective and subjective, and other polarities of human experience.

Psychoanalysis marked the beginning move toward the integration of the nonrational. The Western world, involved in the Industrial Revolution and the romanticization of the "scientific" and the "objective," associated the realms of nonobjective reality with all that was regressive, primitive, infantile, and foolish. However, psychoanalysis itself attempted to fit the "scientific objective" context in order to obtain respectability. (Carl Jung's "mystical" ideas caused a major split in the early psychoanalytic movement, but, like psychodrama, they have become increasingly recognized over the past few years as being relevant to the needs of our contemporary culture.)

During the second half of the twentieth century, the technological-philosophical pendulum has begun to swing back again toward an incorporation of the dimensions of emotion, sensation and imagination into the world of personal experience. The excesses and oversaturation of technological and objective consciousness are being recognized. For example, the concept of psychotherapy is no longer being restricted to the modes of dyadic or group verbal discussion. A "new eclecticism" which includes action in psychotherapy is being increasingly accepted. Moreover, changes in the field of psychotherapy, the phenomena of encounter groups, improvisation in theater and music, and innovations in education exemplify the trend toward the experiential mode of involvement.

The importance of these phenomena was foretold fifty years ago by Jacob L. Moreno, a Viennese psychiatrist who developed

the methods of sociometry and psychodrama, as well as being
a major contributor to the evolution of group psychotherapy.
In an effort to reintroduce the spirit of growth-through-play into
our lives, he emphasized ideas about spontaneity, creativity, action, self-disclosure and risk-taking in "encounter," importance of the present (he coined the term "here-and-now"), the
significance of touch and nonverbal communication, the cultivation of imagination and intuition, and the value of humor and the
depth of drama. The psychodramatic method and its derivatives
are the primary vehicles by which people can learn to develop
these potentialities in themselves.

CAUTIONS

At this point, I wish to note some cautions for the reader.
Psychodrama is no panacea: any romanticizing of a single
approach is dangerous, as it blinds one to the limits of that
approach and the values of other methods. Psychodramatic
techniques can be very powerful, and it behooves the practitioner
to develop his skills with humility and commitment. The therapist
or group leader must be helped to build a broad armamentarium
of skills and a depth of ability with which to apply them, for
mere technique is not enough. With creativity and sensitivity,
the practitioner must learn to know and work with the psychological dimensions of his client's life.

I would strongly encourage the reader to obtain some supervised
training in the use of psychodrama before attempting to apply
any but the most elementary methods. The mastery of psychodrama itself requires a significantly greater degree of training than
can be described in any one book. One cannot learn these
approaches through "cookbook" reading, any more than one can
learn art or music. Nevertheless, I hope that the reader may
be stimulated to use some of the methods, and to continue to
explore the theories and applications of an eclectic approach to
psychotherapy and education. I further emphasize the importance of supplemental readings from the annotated bibliography
at the end of this book.

In summary, therefore, I am presenting this book as an introduction to the theory and practice of using the psychodramatic method in a wide variety of psychotherapeutic and educational settings. I believe that the applications of these methods can do much to facilitate the reintroduction of the elements of spontaneity and creative empathy into human experience.

References

Abroms, Gene. The new eclecticism. *Archives of General Psychiatry,* 1969, *20*, 514-523.

Blatner, Howard A. Comments on some commonly held reservations about psychodrama. *Group Psychotherapy,* 1968, *21* (1), 20-23.

Bromberg, Walter. Acting and acting out. *American Journal of Psychotherapy,* 1958, *12*, 264-268.

Clements, Cooper C. Acting out vs acting through: An interview with Frederick Perls, *Voices,* 1968

Fingarette, Herbert. Self deception in R.F. Holland (Ed.) *Studies in philosophical psychology.* New York: Humanities Press, 1969.

Hillman, James. *Insearch: Psychology and religion.* New York: Charles Scribners Sons, 1967.

Kreitler, Hans and Eblinger, Shulamith. Psychiatric and cultural aspects of the opposition to psychodrama. *Group Psychotherapy,* 1961, *14*, 215-220.

Ormont, Louis R. Acting-in and the therapeutic contract in group psychoanalysis. *International Journal of Group Psychotherapy,* October 1969, *19*, 420-432.

Roszak, Theodore. *The making of a counter-culture.* New York: Doubleday, 1969.

Schwartz, Leonard and Schwartz, R. Therapeutic acting-out. *Psychotherapy: Theory, Research and Practice,* 1971, *8*(3), 205-207.

Zeligs, M.A. Acting-in. *Journal of American Psychoanalytic Association,* 1957, *5*, 685-706.

1

The Basic Elements
of Psychodrama

Psychodrama is the method by which a person can be helped to explore the psychological dimensions of his problems through the *enactment* of his conflict situations, rather than by talking about them. The methods derived from psychodrama can be applied and modified in a wide variety of settings. Although psychodrama and its related methods have much in common with the dynamics of psychotherapy and group-centered education, the terminology in this book will relate to the essentially *dramaturgical* nature of the process. Some of the more common terms will be noted below.

The *protagonist* is the term for the person who is the subject of the psychodramatic enactment. Whether he be acting as a client, patient, student, trainee, group member, or other form of participant, when a person portrays his own life situation he is the protagonist.

The *director* is the person who guides the protagonist in the use of the psychodramatic method in order to help the protagonist explore his problem. The director may be the person in the group who is ordinarily considered to be the group leader, therapist, teacher, or counselor.

The *auxiliary ego,* or simply the *auxiliary,* is the term for anyone besides the protagonist and the director who takes part in a psychodrama. Uusally the auxiliary ego portrays someone in the protagonist's life, such as a wife, employer, or another part of the protagonist himself. Some of the special roles and techniques which can be played by the auxiliary include the *double* and the *antagonist;* these are discussed further in Chapters 2 and 3.

The *audience* refers to the others present during the psychodrama. The audience may be the psychotherapy group, a seminar or class in school, or other members of the protagonist's family. Unlike a conventional audience, the audience in psychodrama often takes an active role in participating in the protagonist's exploration of his feelings.

THE VEHICLES OF PSYCHODRAMA

The *stage* is the area in which the enactment takes place. The stage may be a formal platform for psychodrama; it may be the area in the middle of a group; or the actual locus of the conflict

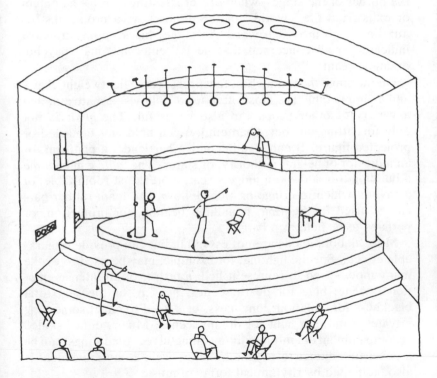

Figure 1

in situ (e.g., the re-enactment and exploration of a conflict between children on the playground where it was occurring earlier). There are some props and structures, however, which can make the dramatic function even more effective.

In the original form of psychodrama, a stage such as that shown in Figure 1 was used. The three levels, lighting arrangements, balcony, and design were all empirically developed to facilitate the power of the enactments. Any of these components can be useful if included.

The main stage should be at least approximately 12-15 feet in diameter. A raised platform which can easily be stepped onto is helpful in subliminally establishing the "as-if" set in the participant. (The Greeks used the term "proscenium arch" to mark the border of the stage—when one crosses the "arch" he enters or exits from the "world" of the drama.) As a protagonist or auxiliary ego moves toward the stage, his stepping upward indicates to all concerned that he is "entering" his "psycho-dramatic reality."

On the stage there may be a few props: some lightweight chairs and a simple table are most often used. Pillows, a mattress, and a variety of other props can also be useful. The *chair* is not only for sitting on, but when empty, can hold any fantasied or projected figure. It can also become a barricade, a platform, or an indicator of height, authority, or status. The *table* can become a building-top, a desk, a judge's seat, a breakfast-room table, or a cave in which to cringe or hide. Pillows and foam rubber bats can be used for fighting, pounding, beating, for protection, or perhaps to be held as a baby.

More elaborate aids are not essential, but can provide remarkable effects. Special lighting, for example, may be used to evoke many moods: red to represent hell, a bistro, or an intense emotional scene; blue for death scenes, heaven, or the sea; total blackness for isolation, loneliness, or a need to enact something privately; and dim light for dream scenes. Music, either skilled accompaniment or emotionally-meaningful recorded songs, can be a powerful adjunct to psychodrama as well. Body movement is also facilitated by rhythmical forms of music.

MAJOR FORMS OF PSYCHODRAMATIC ENACTMENT

Psychodrama refers to an enactment involving emotional problem-solving in terms of *one person's* conflict; it is "protagonist-centered." The drama may shift among the many facets of the protagonist's life—his past, present, and future. Usually psychodrama moves toward relatively deep emotional issues.

Psychodrama as a form of psychotherapy was originated around 1920 by Dr. Moreno, who then went on to develop many modifications which would be appropriate for a variety of group situations.

Sociodrama is a form of psychodramatic enactment which aims at clarifying *group* themes rather than focusing on the individual's problems. Although a person may participate as a protagonist in a sociodrama, the focus of the group task is on the problems of the *role* he plays in the drama rather than on his personal life situation. Thus sociodrama could be termed *group-centered*.

A group of nurses in training, for example, might use sociodrama to explore the challenge of dealing with certain kinds of patients. When one of the nurses (as the protagonist) becomes involved in a scene, the emotional issues of the problem will be expressed. However, the director should bring out those facets of the relationship which would likely be present in many or *most* nurse-patient interactions; those feelings unique to the protagonist would *not* be emphasized. In other words, it would be inappropriate in a sociodrama for a director to deal with the *personal* aspects of the nurse who is the protagonist, for this might imply to the others in the group that the difficulties in the interaction were due to deficiencies unique to that nurse.

A sociodrama can function as a *warm-up* for a protagonist-centered psychodrama in settings where exploration of the individual's life is part of the group task. Sociodrama, however, is sufficient in itself as a modality for exploring the stresses involved in the relationships between police and citizen, parent and child, boy and girl, customer and salesman, different races, employer and employee, or student and teacher.

Role-playing, like sociodrama, is a derivative of psychodrama. Although some people use all these terms interchangeably, most professionals would consider role-playing to be more superficial and problem-oriented. Expression of deep feelings is not usually part of most role-playing operations. Rather, the goal of role-playing tends to be working out alternative and more effective approaches to a general problem. Industry, school, and professional training contexts are more likely to utilize this modality in meeting tasks such as developing interviewing skills, dealing with difficult children, handling customer relations, etc.

Psychodramatic techniques, used in a variety of contexts, are also known by terms such as *action methods, encounter techniques, growth games, theater games, structured experiences,* or *nonverbal exercises.* Although many of these techniques were originated by Dr. Moreno and other psychodramatists, many ideas have also been modified from the fields of guided fantasy, psychosynthesis, sensory awakening, Gestalt Therapy, Bioenergetics, improvisatory dramatics, and other related methods. Whatever their origin, psychodramatic techniques can be applied in many situations where formal psychodrama, sociodrama, or role-playing might not be appropriate. Indeed, one of the chief aims of this book is to encourage the reader to begin to experiment with the use of psychodramatic methods first, and then to practice the more complex approaches.

THE TECHNIQUES OF PSYCHODRAMA

Scores of psychodramatic techniques exist, along with hundreds of variations and modifications. Most of the major techniques are described in different sections of this book. These techniques can be used in order to accomplish a variety of goals.

In order to *clarify a protagonist's feelings,* the techniques of *the double, soliloquy, multiple selves,* and *monodrama* are used.

For heightening and facilitating the *expression of emotion*, the director may use *amplification, asides,* and the exaggerations of nonverbal communications, along with exaggerations of the dimensions of height, space, and position.

The protagonist may be aided in becoming aware of his own

behavior *(self-confrontation)* through the use of techniques such as *videotape playback, role reversal, behind-your-back, audience feedback, chorus,* and *nonverbal interaction exercises.*

Goals and values may be clarified through the use of the *magic shop* or the *future-projection techniques.*

Support can be given with the techniques of *ego-building, sharing,* and the judicious use of *physical contact,* such as hugging or holding.

Issues of *group process* can be clarified through the techniques of the *spectrogram* and *sociometry.*

Finally, there are many special techniques which can be used along with psychodrama, such as *hypnosis* and *guided fantasy.*

Through the use of the above-mentioned techniques, the director can help the protagonist to enact the range of his experiences: scenes from everyday life, as well as his dreams, memories, delusions, fears, and fantasies.

AN OUTLINED DESCRIPTION OF A TYPICAL PSYCHODRAMATIC ENACTMENT

I. The Warm-up (see Chapter 4)

    A. The director warms himself up.

    B. The group discusses goals, roles, fees, limits, time arrangements, etc.

    C. Getting acquainted; exercises are used which introduce group members to each other.

    D. The director leads the group in action exercises which build group cohesion and spontaneity.

    E. This often leads to a discussion of what the participant experienced in the warm-up exercises, which in turn leads to the emergence of a theme of common interest to the group, or to an individual's problem.

    F. One of the group members is selected to be the protagonist, who will enact his own or the group's problem.

II. The Action (see Chapter 5)

    A. The director brings the protagonist to the stage, where the problem is briefly discussed.

B. The conflict is re-defined in terms of a concrete example —one that could be *enacted*.

C. The director helps the protagonist to describe the setting in which a specific action occurs, thus "setting the stage."

D. The protagonist is instructed to play the scene as if it were occurring in the "here-and-now."

E. The director brings other members of the group forward to take the parts of other significant figures in the protagonist's drama—these people then become the *auxiliary egos*.

F. The opening scene is portrayed.

G. The director helps the auxiliary egos to learn their roles by having the protagonist change parts with them (reverse roles) for a brief period during which the protagonist then portrays the behavior of the other figures in his drama. As the auxiliaries learn their roles, the protagonist gives them feedback until he feels that the scene is being enacted in an essentially similar way to the way he pictures it in his mind. This "molding" activity furthers the warm-up of the auxiliary egos and the protagonist himself.

H. The scene continues with the director introducing other psychodramatic techniques which function to elaborate on the feelings being expressed (e.g., soliloquy, the double technique, asides, etc.)

I. As the enactment unfolds, the director uses a variety of other techniques in order to explore different facets of the protagonist's experience.

   1. Ambivalence is explicitly demonstrated through the use of several individuals (auxiliaries) on the stage, each portraying a different part of the protagonist's psyche.

   2. Empathetic or projected feelings of the protagonist can be enacted through role reversal.

   3. Self-confrontation for the protagonist may be utilized through the *mirror technique*.

   4. Significant past memories are re-enacted.

      5. Future plans, hopes, and fears can be symbolically realized and explored.

      6. The protagonist's suppressed emotions—guilts, resentments, fears, yearning—can all be expressed using a variety of facilitating techniques.

J. The action may be carried to a point where the protagonist experiences a sense of having symbolically enacted those behaviors which had been suppressed—fulfillment of *act hunger*.

K. The protagonist is helped to develop other adaptive attitudinal and behavioral responses to his situation—this is called *working through* (see Chapter 6). (In role-playing contexts, this process may become the predominant task of the group.) Some specific techniques used in working through include:

      1. Repeat role-playing of the conflict, with the protagonist trying a different approach with each attempt.

      2. Modeling by other group members, to show how *they* would deal with the problem.

      3. Role reversal between the protagonist and his antagonists—the other figures in his enactment—so that the protagonist can discover, through actually *experiencing* the other person's situation, some clues as to what behaviors might achieve the desired effect.

III. Closure (see Chapter 6)

A. Following the main action, the director helps the protagonist to receive some supportive feedback from the other group members. Rather than encouraging an intellectualized analysis of the protagonist's problem, the director encourages the group members to *share* with the protagonist the feelings they had related to the enactment.

B. The director may proceed to use a variety of supportive psychodramatic techniques.

C. Further discussion by the group ensues.

D. Finally, the director either goes on to the process of warming-up to another psychodramatic enactment with a different protagonist, or moves toward terminating the group, possibly using a variety of *closing techniques*.

2

The Auxiliary Ego

The auxiliary ego, sometimes simply called the auxiliary, is the term used for any person other than the director who participates in a psychodramatic enactment in order to help the protagonist explore his problem. Auxiliary egos play a variety of roles not only in psychodramatic, sociodramatic, and role-playing situations, but they also can be used as an action technique in ongoing psychotherapy or development groups.

TYPES OF AUXILIARY EGO ROLES

The role of a significant other person, someone in the protagonist's *social atom,** e.g., a wife, son, employer, friend, therapist, etc. When this person is the main character in the enactment playing opposite the protagonist, he is occasionally called *the antagonist.*

The double, the auxiliary who takes the role of the protagonist's *alter ego.* In this role, the auxiliary ego as double helps the protagonist to express his inner feelings more clearly. The technique of using an auxiliary in the role of double is extremely important in psychodrama, and will be discussed more fully in the next chapter.

The part of someone more distant, in a general role—a policeman, teacher, client—but no specific person personally known to the protagonist (this is more commonly used in sociodrama and has a rather peripheral role in a psychodrama).

Social Atom: Moreno's term for the complex of all the significant figures, real and fantasied, past and present, who relate to a person's psychological experience.

The role of a fantasied figure, e.g. God, a judge, a tempter, an idealized father the protagonist never knew, the "Prince Charming" who will rescue the protagonist.

An inanimate object to which the protagonist relates, e.g., his bed, doorway, house, the desk that mocks its owner (the protagonist) for his lack of self-discipline: "Hey! What about all this work you've piled on me? You're always saying you'll get to me, but you never do!"

An example of this would be that of a woman who, exploring her relationship with her daughter-in-law, acts the part of her daughter's-in-law living room. "It" becomes embarrassed when the "mother-in-law" pays a visit, and says in an aside to the audience: "Oh-oh, here she comes . . . she's going to want to change everything!" Then, to the mother-in-law: "Don't you think I could possibly look good unless you have a hand in fixing me up?"

The role of an abstract concept or a collective stereotype, e.g., "they," "society," "contemporary youth," "the church," "justice," etc.

FUNCTIONS OF THE AUXILIARY EGO

The auxiliary ego helps the protagonist to explore his situation by acting toward him in the role assigned: the employer who behaves in a "calling-on-the-carpet" manner, the mother who worries or infantilizes, the spouse who argues but doesn't listen.

The performance of this role must be similar in essence to the behavior of the person being represented, but need not be exact. Indeed, a small amount of unexpected behavior on the part of the auxiliary ego often increases the protagonist's spontaneous involvement in coping with that challenge.

The auxiliary ego's behavior evokes a similar response: if the auxiliary whispers, the protagonist tends to respond as if there were a secret; if the auxiliary "escalates" into screaming and cursing, this may bring out a similar expressiveness on the protagonist's part. (This is called a "symmetric" response.)

The auxiliary ego's role may stimulate the protagonist to take a "complementary" role: if the auxiliary acts judgmental, the protagonist responds with defensiveness, rebelliousness, or he gives an explanation; if the auxiliary acts helpless, the protagonist becomes protective. In the same way, dominance provokes submissiveness, etc.

The auxiliary ego's speaking in the "here-and-now" and his manner of encountering "in-role" tends to pull the protagonist into the interaction as if it were actually happening there for the first time. Thus the auxiliary functions to involve the protagonist more deeply in the psychodramatic enactment, which in turn tends to bring out his basic conflicts and suppressed feelings more rapidly and completely.

There are times, however, when the protagonist ought to play all the parts in the enactment himself. The drama with no auxiliary egos is called *autodrama* or *monodrama*. The protagonist may shift places using one or two empty chairs, and have an encounter between different parts of himself, or with his projection of someone with whom he has a conflict. Fritz Perls used monodrama as a core technique in Gestalt Therapy.

Some of the indications for the directors choosing to use monodrama instead of using auxiliary egos include:

when the protagonist is in individual therapy;

when the director wants the protagonist to find out that the "answers" to his questions are to be found within himself;

when the protagonist could play both roles in an encounter much easier than could any auxiliary ego.

THE SELECTION OF THE AUXILIARY EGO

The role of the auxiliary ego is usually played either by one of the group members or by a *professional auxiliary ego*. The professional or trained auxiliary is most often found in situations where there is an ongoing program of psychodrama. He may be a psychodrama director-in-training, a nurse on an in-patient ward, a co-therapist or simply another staff member who is experienced in the use of psychodramatic methods.

The main advantage of using a professional auxiliary ego to play key roles is that he is experienced in warming himself up to the roles involved. An auxiliary who can play a variety of roles and easily express feelings (i.e., one who has a high degree of spontaneity) can galvanize a psychodramatic enactment. Furthermore, a great deal of spontaneity is especially necessary in roles which involve the exhibition of grossly crude, childish, cruel, arrogant, "bitchy," seductive, or humiliating behavior.

On the other hand, even when there are trained auxiliary egos present, there are times when it is best to allow different group members to be auxiliaries and play the various parts.

For example, in a psychodrama in which a girl is exploring her competitive feelings toward other women, the auxiliary ego who is to be the man over whom the girls fight may be played by one of the shy men in the group. While his role as auxiliary serves a function in the girl's exploration of her problem, it may also benefit him. Even in warm-up techniques, group members may be picked to play parts which would normally oppose their habitual style: the constricted, "nice-guy" type might benefit by acting in the role of a "villain"; the shy, plain girl may discover some sexy aspects of herself by playing a "seductress"; a "stuffed shirt" may loosen up by playing a role which gives him permission to be silly, i.e., a child, a monster, or an animal.

Another factor to be considered in the selection of auxiliary egos is the degree to which a group member identifies with the protagonist's situation, or with the position of one of the other parts in the enactment. If an auxiliary ego has a conflict in his own life which is similar to that of the protagonist, the value the psychodrama has for the protagonist can either be increased or decreased. To some extent the "carry-over" from the auxiliary's own situation can validly be applied to the protagonist's life, but beyond that it can become a disconcerting pressure which only confuses the protagonist. Unless the director is alert to the auxiliary ego's behavior and applies firm control, the auxiliary can impose artificial issues upon the protagonist's drama. The director may occasionally check with the protagonist by asking: "Is this the way your wife, mother, etc., acts?"

TECHNIQUES IN THE SELECTION OF THE AUXILIARY EGO

Most often the director asks the protagonist to choose the auxiliary for specific roles. It may be useful to later ask the protagonist to examine the determinants for his "intuitive" choice.

The professional *auxiliary,* often staff members or experienced group members, is chosen by the director.

The director may choose a group member to be an auxiliary because he believes either that the auxiliary would benefit, that the auxiliary could play the role well, that the auxiliary has familiarity with the role, or that the role is so narrowly defined that there would be only one person in the group who could either play or identify with that role.

The director may ask for suggestions from the group as to which member should take each role.

The director may ask for volunteers, for any who are empathetic and have a desire to play a specific auxiliary role: "Has anyone here been in Joe's situation and could 'double' with him?"

After an enactment the auxiliary is often asked not only to "share" his own feelings regarding the protagonist's situation, but is also invited to comment on his own experiences "in-role" as an auxiliary ego.

As an example, in an ongoing psychodramatically-oriented therapy group I conducted for Stanford University for two years, one young man (let us call him Bob) had difficulty participating in the first several sessions. Bob was about 23 years of age, shy, constricted, intellectualized, and lonely. During one session in which another group member, an attractive girl, was enacting an attempted rape which had happened to her the previous week, Bob was chosen to be the auxiliary ego who would play the "rapist." The scene was dramatic, menacing, and full of physical activity as Bob enacted the partial overpowering of the girl. Although discreet limits were observed (somehow the absorption of the players is rarely so total as to allow their behaviors to go beyond the boundaries of group norms, i.e., being violent) there was nevertheless a good deal of wrestling in the scene. After the enactment, the catching of breath, and a period of sharing with the girl who was the protagonist, I turned to Bob and asked him how he felt about the scene. "I liked it," he replied with surprising candor and a smug smile. Over the next several sessions, Bob was given several role situations in which he expressed competitiveness, sexual domination, submissiveness, exuberance, anger, and fear. Following a period of time, he dramatically changed his passive, introverted style to include active, extroverted behavior as part of his life pattern.

Another technique is for the director to ask the group members, after an enactment, to discuss roles in which they would be most or least comfortable. The group could also discuss which roles would be most helpful for each to play in the future. These discussions further help the group members to develop receptivity towards playing the auxiliary ego role in later enactments.

OTHER AUXILIARY EGO ROLES

The auxiliary chair   An empty chair can be used in a warm-up (see Chapter 4, p. 45), and can also represent the significant other in an enactment. If the protagonist feels angry, he may beat the chair with cushions or kick the chair—actions he would not be permitted to perform with a "live" auxiliary ego. The chair can

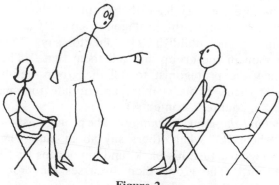

Figure 2

also be a barrier to get around, representing either an emotional or physical block. Lastly, two empty chairs are often used as props for the protagonist to move to and from. For example (see Figure 2), the director says: "Joe, in this chair, the nice, obedient part of you speaks to your mother (played by an auxiliary); in that chair, the rebellious, sullen part of you can also talk to your mother in a way you have never expressed yourself."

The silent auxiliary ego   There are times when it is sufficient to keep an auxiliary ego on stage even if he is to be silent, for he can provide support simply by being present.

THE AUDIENCE AUXILIARY EGO

Members of the audience can be asked to give comments, either in the discussion period or during a break in the enactment. Sometimes specific roles will be assigned: someone to "observe" the process; someone to "identify with" the protagonist and/or one of the auxiliary's roles; someone to try to think of alternate solutions.

Several group members may chant or repeat some fixed statement in the background as a chorus, such as the contents of a hallucination, obsession, delusion, judgment attitude, secret wish, etc.

The audience may be used as objects of the protagonist's statements: the protagonist makes a statement reflecting an internalized attitude, the director may have that attitude "played out" until it becomes hollow, e.g., the protagonist says, "I am an adult," but continues to act childish. The director says, "Go around to each person in the group and tell them that." The director may also ask the protagonist to tell the group members what he thinks of them. (This is more appropriate for small group therapy in "encounter" contexts.)

Using behind-the-back technique   The protagonist may benefit from "overhearing" what others say about him. The director has the protagonist turn his back, and announces that he is "no longer present." The group then discusses the protagonist as if he were not in the room.

Audience members can double for each other, and speak out on issues where they might otherwise be silent. A trained auxiliary ego might start this, and the others follow. For example: the audience is getting bored, but says nothing. An audience double exaggerates the group's slouching, nonverbal behavior and shouts, "Boy, is this boring!" or "He's manipulating the heck out of us!"

GUIDELINES FOR THE AUXILIARY EGOS

The many techniques whereby the director can involve the auxiliaries are known as "warming-up" the auxiliary ego. Much of what is said about warming-up in Chapter 4 applies here. These techniques also apply to the warming-up of the double (see Chapter 3).

At the outset of the enactment, the protagonist can "role-reverse" (i.e., change parts) and demonstrate the behavior that the auxiliary ego is to portray. The protagonist may state the opening lines spoken by both parties. The director can then ask the protagonist in the role of the other person to show not only the other's words, but also the other person's mood, posture, tone of voice, and nonverbal behavior.

From the moment the auxiliary is selected, he should be encouraged to move right into the role, acting in the here-and-now.

For example, if a group member is picked to be the protagonist's mother, she may begin talking even as she moves onto the stage: "Look at you! You're so thin! Doesn't your wife feed you?"

The auxiliary should play his hunches, take risks, and follow the cues of the director and the protagonist. If the protagonist corrects him, the auxiliary should change set quickly, e.g.,

Protagonist: No, my mother is different, she only talks about herself.

Auxiliary Ego (changing set): Oh, Bill, why haven't you written me?! You know how lonely I am. . . .

Protagonist (nods his head, and answers): "But Mom . . .

As the scene changes or parts are reversed, the auxiliary ego is instructed to repeat the last spoken line in his role, e.g.,

Protagonist (as mother): Why haven't you written?

Auxiliary ego (as protagonist): Well . . .

Director. (interrupting, to let protagonist answer for himself): Change parts. (They change places on the stage.)

Auxiliary Ego as mother (repeats last line): Why haven't you written?

Protagonist: Mom, I wrote you last month!

Auxiliary Ego (carrying on): Last month is too long, etc.

The director should consider briefing the auxiliary ego as to his role, or have the protagonist brief the auxiliary to the side while the director keeps the attention of the group.

Smoking should be prohibited on stage in order to free the participants' hands for dramatic gesture or action.

The auxiliary can be asked to bring up his own chair or prop, thus mobilizing his activity.

The auxiliary can be helped by yet another auxiliary who doubles for him; this technique thus warms up the auxiliary ego.

The auxiliary ego should be told to follow the director's directions, which may be spoken out loud or whispered to him.

If the protagonist tends to drop out-of-role, the auxiliary should address him as if he were still "in-role:" "How dare you turn your back on your mother!" The auxiliary may even grab the protagonist's arm.

The protagonist should be checked with occasionally to see if the auxiliary ego is playing the scene with reasonable accuracy. If the auxiliary cannot satisfy the protagonist's sense of how the role is to be played, the director should feel free to dismiss the auxiliary and use someone else.

A scene can be staged which precedes the main scene in time or logical sequence, e.g., the "employer" plays a brief scene in which he receives information from another auxiliary, the "foreman," about the "employee" regarding the protagonist's difficulties in work; following this, the confrontation between protagonist and employer can be staged.

Further guidelines can be found in the works of Seabourne, Moreno, Haskell and Corsini.

SUMMARY

The auxiliary ego's function is to play a variety of roles in the protagonist's enactment. The auxiliary's behavior and confrontation provoke the protagonist into a deeper involvement in the here-and-now of the drama. The effective use of the auxiliary ego can heighten the power of any action approach.

References

Corsini, Raymond J. Behind your back technique. *Group Psychotherapy,* 1954, *6,* 102-109.

Loeffler, F. J. and Weinstein, H. M. The co-therapist method: Problems and advantages. *Group Psychotherapy,* 1954, *6,* 189.

Moreno, Zerka Toeman. The auxiliary ego, double, and mirror techniques. *Sociometry,* 1946, *9,* 178.

Moreno, Zerka T. Reluctant audience technique. *Group Psychotherapy,* 1958, *11*(1), 278-282.

Perls, Frederick S. *Gestalt therapy verbatim.* Lafayette, Calif.: Real People Press, 1969.

Rosenberg, Pearl Pollock. An experimental analysis of psychodrama. Unpublished doctoral dissertaion, Harvard University, 1952.

Seabourne, Barbara. The role of the auxiliary. Unpublished manuscript, St. Louis State Hospital, 1966.

3

The Double

The double technique consists of the use of an auxiliary ego in the specialized role of playing the part of the inner self of the protagonist. The double is occasionally called the *alter ego* by some directors. Because the expression of the protagonist's deepest emotions can be one of the major purposes of the use of psychodramatic methods, and because the use of the double is the most effective technique in bringing out emotions, this technique may well be called "the heart of psychodrama."

FUNCTIONS

In general the purpose of the double is to stimulate interaction by facilitating the portrayal of the protagonist's psychological experience to its fullest range. This function may be fulfilled in many ways, which will be described later.

A second major function is to provide support for the protagonist, which helps him to take more risks and enter the interaction more completely.

A third function of the double technique is to be a vehicle for giving more effective suggestions and interpretations to the protagonist. If the auxiliary playing the double role has built a "bridge" of rapport through his behavior, the protagonist is relatively open to accepting and considering statements made by the double as if part of his own self were speaking. Of course, it is imperative that the director establish the norm in which the protagonist is free to disagree with, modify, or expand on the double's statement.

This "empathy" function of doubling can be used in many settings. For example, in individual or family therapy, I may present an "interpretation-of-sorts" in the following format:

"I may not be right, but I have a hunch of what you may be experiencing in that situation . . . now I'm going to be you, (John, the protagonist) and speak what you may be feeling—but you must correct me as to how it can be closer to what you're feeling . . ." (then I go into the content): "Here I am reading my paper and Sandy barges in—that really irritates me!" etc.

This is equivalent to my "role-reversing" with the protagonist, without expecting him to take my role. I call it "active empathy"—it's very like Rogerian feedback, only somewhat dramatized. Instead of saying, "I'm hearing that you're feeling . . . ," the therapist becomes the protagonist and then invites the protagonist to correct the "performance." This approach can be readily adapted to family therapy.

THE TECHNIQUE OF THE DOUBLE

The double is selected in the same way as the other auxiliary egos (see Chapter 2). The director introduces the double to the protagonist as follows:

"Consider this person your double, your invisible self, your alter ego with whom you may talk at times, but who exists only within yourself. He may say things that you may be feeling—things you would be hesitant to express. If his statements represent your true feelings, repeat that statement in your interaction. (See example, Chapter 5. p. 58).

"If what the double says is not an expression of your feelings, you are free to correct him, to say 'no.' This will negate what he says. He is then to try to better approximate your emotional state, and will try to help you express your feelings and thoughts more openly. If you, the protagonist, feel the double is unable to empathize with you, you may indicate this, and we will replace him."

The director may use either of two minor variations of the technique: (1) only the protagonist may respond to what the double says, and if the double's statement is to be answered by the other people in the drama, the protagonist must repeat it; or (2) what the double says is spoken so that all may hear and it may be considered an open expression of the protagonist's feelings, unless specifically contradicted by the protagonist.

The former variant, in which the protagonist must repeat the double's statements, reinforces the necessity for the protagonist to take responsibility for what transpires, and is indicated for use with more passive protagonists. The latter variant, in which what the double says may be answered directly by the others, has the advantage of speeding up the interaction.

As with the role of the auxiliary ego, there is no requirement that the person chosen to play the double resemble the actual person he portrays. "There is no age, sex, status, or race in psychodrama," says Moreno. (It is true that protagonists often pick people who resemble the "real" person for auxiliary ego parts, but this is not necessary.) Under any circumstances, if the auxiliary behaves even somewhat "true to role," the protagonist fully accepts him "in-role"—as mother, wife, or double.

If there is role reversal in the enactment, the double should take on whatever role the protagonist is involved in. Throughout the enactment the double should continue to speak in the first person: "I think," "I feel . . ." and never (to the protagonist) "you think . . ."

KINDS OF DOUBLING

In helping to express emotions, the double can emphasize or "amplify" statements made by the protagonist. If the double stresses that the protagonist is feeling something strongly, but is not expressing those affects, the double may speak out and ventilate the anger, love, or whatever is experienced.

A good example of this occurred during a multiple-family therapy group at a community mental health center where a daughter lashed out at her father, accusing him of being unfair and stating that she hated him. He trembled, but with his characteristic efforts at self-control, responded "Why do you hate me?" The double stood behind him and shouted, "You damn bitch! You're humiliating me! I'm trying to be controlled, but, oh, that hurt! I want you to love me!" At this, the father wept and agreed with the double, and the interaction proceeded at a more intense pace. Other ways of doubling are as follows:

Dramatizing the feelings   An extension of the first approach of doubling is the principle of maximizing the emotional content of an attitude. Thus if the protagonist says, "I like you," the double can say, "I need you"; "I'm irritated" becomes, "I hate you." Obviously, this approach should be used only when it seems that the maximizing expression is either accurate or would be productive in clarifying the protagonist's feelings.

Verbalizing nonverbal communications   Here the double begins to add more "content" to the self-system of the protagonist. If the protagonist smiles ingratiatingly, the double responds, "Why must I smile when I speak to him?" A tense jaw or clenched fist may be verbalized as, "This is getting me angry."

Physicalizing words and gestures   The double extends himself to hug, cling, shove, or push the other auxiliary egos in the interaction. He may strike a pillow, cringe in a crouching position, or stand on a chair to speak. This is dramatization in the nonverbal sphere.

Support   The double reinforces the protagonist's right to his feelings: "Dammit! Why should I live up to your expectations?" or, "I don't buy that load of crap!"; "It's okay if I *feel* like this!"

Questioning the self   The double questions the protagonist's attitude; again, this must be used with discretion: "Maybe I'm kidding myself . . ." or, "Is that how I really feel?"

Contradicting the feelings   The double contradicts the protagonist, but only if he wants to evoke a reinforced statement or if he believes the protagonist's self-system includes a stance opposite to his statement: "Y'know, I don't really feel this way at all!"; "I don't hate you . . . I need you!"; or, "I hate you *and* I love you!"

Defending against the feelings   The double actively verbalizes the paradigms of the protagonist's habitual defense mechanisms:

Denial: "This can't be happening!" Isolation: "I don't feel a thing." Projection: "I would never feel towards you the way you feel toward me." Displacement: "Dammit! Someone's got to take the blame!!" etc.

Self-observation   The double notes the protagonist's general situation by introducing some comment on the protagonist's behavior: "I seem to be getting more tense"; "Oh-oh, I'm explaining again."

Related to this is the noting of emotions in the here-and-now: "I'm talking about the past, but I'm feeling embarrassed now." The double can also act as a counselor: "Say . . . I'm reacting as if he's judging me!"

Interpretation   The double must be very sensitive in his introduction of materials which are outside the protagonist's awareness. Commenting on what is *not* being said is one form: "I'm not saying anything about Dad . . . just talking to Mom!" Referring to past incidents or other issues is another form of interpretation: "I used to feel this way as a kid!"

Interpretation of carry-over to other relationships   An important variable to be remembered is that at times the protagonist is responding to those in his enactment on two levels: not only in terms of who the other person as auxiliary is portraying (father, employer, etc.), but also in terms of who the auxiliary is in real life. For example, if the auxiliary role of father is being played by the person who is also the protagonist's therapist in other settings, the statements of the protagonist may reflect not only feelings toward the father, but also feelings toward the therapist. (This is a kind of reverse transference.) For example, in one session, the protagonist was expressing a series of demands to his "father." The double then added:—and I'm not only saying this to you as my father, but also as my *therapist!*" This led to the protagonist's agreement and a further shift of scene towards a re-evaluation of the therapist-patient relationship.

This kind of doubling can be applied to the generalization of other feelings, irrespective of who plays the other auxiliary roles: e.g.: "I'm frightened of you . . . I'm frightened of everybody!" or "I've felt this way with all women!"

Satire   The use of humor in psychotherapy and in doubling may be one of the most delicate arts, but at times can be very effective: "Yeah, I *want* it! I want love *and* guarantees *and* obedience!" or, "Of course I don't resent it! I like being put down!"

The use of satire, opposition, and provocation in doubling can add power to an enactment if used with sensitivity and the proper timing. Without the "art," the use of "shock" only leads to dissonance. The stubborn double who believes that he is making "an interpretation" when he repeatedly reinforces his statement to the repeated denials by his protagonist is only making a fool of himself or hurting his protagonist.

Divided double   Here the double is assigned to play a specific role or part of the protagonist's psyche, usually made explicit by the director. The double may be the "obedient" or the "defiant" part; the "self-blaming" or the "externalizing, self-justifying" part. This frees the protagonist to clarify his feelings about the other complementary attitudes. In this technique the director may have more than one double for different parts of the protagonist. Thus two or three doubles may be on stage.

Multiple doubles   The director may allow several people to express their feelings to the protagonist as doubles. Whereas the auxiliary as a *divided double* plays one "complex" or *part* of the protagonist's psyche, as a *multiple double,* each auxiliary doubles for the protagonist as a whole person. This technique is even more effective in sociodrama, or if the protagonist is enacting an issue that involves others deeply. Again, it must be emphasized that it is still the protagonist's feelings which must be clarified.

An extension of the multiple double is the *group or collective* double: this simply throws the interaction open to the audience and has them shout their double statements (always in the first person tense) from the floor.

The auxiliary's double   Not only can the protagonist have a double, but so may the others in the enactment. On the stage may be the protagonist, his double, his "wife" (played by an auxiliary), *her* double (played by a third auxiliary), and possibly other roles and *their doubles* and so on (see Figure 3).

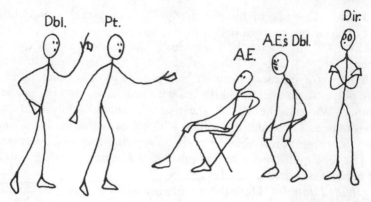

Figure 3

This technique helps those playing the other roles in the enactment to express their feelings more effectively.

Soliloquy   The double can be with the protagonist even when there is no specific interpersonal interaction, i.e., when enacting a soliloquy. Examples would be "on the way home" scenes; "getting ready for bed," or simply walking around the stage with one's double, "talking to oneself out loud."

Doubling for audience   A double may be assigned to help the audience express its feelings, positive or negative, toward the events on the stage or any of the participants in the enactment, including the director.

For example, in a drama that had become "bogged down" in over-intellectualized verbosity, the audience double stood behind some group members and stated, "I'm getting bored . . . I want to help Mary reach out." This approach may catalyze a reaction which, in turn, may further the action in the drama.

Doubling in the warm-up   From the outset, the double can be used to help the protagonist move toward readiness for action on the stage.

For example, the director is talking to a potential protagonist, and the trained auxiliary moves behind that "protagonist" and begins to double: "Say, this is embarrassing, having the director put *me* on the spot . . . I thought I would just observe. . . ."

SOME SUGGESTIONS FOR DOUBLING

The tasks of helping another person to express his feelings may seem imposing, but there are some approaches which can help the potential double in his role. It is not true that an extensive historical background must be understood before one person can make inferences about another's feelings. A great deal of information is easily available from some very obvious cues. The double cannot hope to be absolutely accurate, but he will find that he is empathizing "correctly" in over half the statements he makes if he simply talks about three areas of the protagonist's life: his nonverbal communications, his use of words, and the general roles and role transitions in which the protagonist finds himself. I will describe how the double can draw inferences from these dimensions in this section, and then suggest some exercises which can be used to practice the skill of doubling.

The first group of cues for the double comes from the protagonist's *nonverbal communications*. By imitating the protagonist's posture, expression, gesture and voice tone, the double finds himself experiencing the same kinds of body sensations as his subject. These sensations act as somasthetic cues which provide the double with a wealth of intuitive information about how his subject feels. For example, if a double were to imitate a protagonist who is slumped in his chair, the sensation of the distribution of weight in that posture might suggest to the double the quality of the feeling of his subject (e.g., it might help the double to discern whether the protagonist is sulking, or if he is really depressed). I would suggest that the reader try out the following: unobtrusively imitate others, and to a surprising extent you find yourselves "feeling" as they do.

The best physical position for the double is to place himself behind, slightly to the side of, and facing the protagonist at about a 30 degree angle. From this vantage point he can observe and imitate his subject without being distractingly obvious. The proximity of this position may facilitate a sense of symbolic identification. Rapport may be occasionally heightened by the double's placing one hand on the protagonist's shoulder.

A second source of information for the double may be derived

from the *way the protagonist uses words*. As long as the double
is in the process of trying to understand his subject, he should
try to get a feeling for the protagonist's "self-system." What
kinds of words, what connotations, what levels of abstractions
does the protagonist use? (Some knowledge of semantics is often
very helpful in this regard.) In the early stages of doubling, the
double should try to paraphrase what the protagonist is most
consciously trying to express. Only later, after the rapport has
been established, may he go on to amplify, express, dramatize,
and in other ways extend the doubling to the many functions
noted earlier in this chapter. In the beginning, however, the double
wants to *understand,* and thus needs to listen almost uncritically.
Any caricaturization of the protagonist by the double in the early
phases will disrupt the relationship.

Also based on the protagonist's use of words the double can
find clues as to how his subject is feeling from the *discrepancy
between voice tone and content*. If the protagonist speaks in an
emotion-filled voice about trivial issues, the double may be led
toward thinking about what that emotion means. On the other
hand, if the protagonist is speaking in a flat, effectless tone about
rather dramatic problems, the double may attend to (and later,
comment on) the defense mechanism of isolation of emotion.

The third major technique for the double's building an empathic
awareness of the protagonist is *to assess the protagonist's roles
and obvious characteristics*. These can be divided into several
categories: (1) physical features, (2) stage in life, and (3) the challenges, advantages, and disadvantages of any present or imminent
life roles. The double should assess these obvious or easily acces-
sible conditions. It is not necessary for the double to feel he
must have the "whole story" in order to make inferences about
these roles, since the relationship is such that he can interact
mutually and, if he errs, he can easily be corrected. Nevertheless,
the double will find that a surprisingly high proportion of his
inferences will be accurate. Each accurate response of the double
develops his rapport with the protagonist while an inaccurate
response does *not* alienate him unless it is extreme or humiliating.

For example, an auxiliary ego may make a number of statements
in the double role which might be part of the situation of anyone

who has a physical characteristic which is different from most of the people in his social situation: a different or minority ethnic, racial, or religious affiliation; being tall or short, overweight or thin; having any disfiguring scars or unusual features, and so on. What does a man feel when his hairline begins to recede? What does greying hair mean?

The double can similarly make any comments which would be shared by most people at the following stages in life: the man about to retire; the person being told he has a serious illness; the feelings and anxieties that accompany a promotion; the mixed feelings of being a new parent, and so forth.

Related to the issue of role transition are the groups of feelings which accompany most life roles in the sexual, family, vocational, social, and financial areas. What could any double say about the following situations?: The man who reaches his fiftieth birthday and whose income and status have not met his expectations; the woman in her thirties who finds that her husband has recently been unfaithful; the twenty-two-year-old virgin (male or female); or the young man who feels himself falling into a vocational rut.

The double can thus utilize the inferences which any person can make about a situation or quality, if he would give himself permission to take the risk of playing his hunches out loud.

EXERCISES FOR BUILDING THE CAPACITY FOR DOUBLING

Here are some of the exercises that may be used for building empathic skills; they also are excellent warm-up techniques:

The group breaks into pairs. Each person is instructed to list on a piece of paper four qualities which he likes about himself, and four qualities which he dislikes. After the lists are made, the group members are instructed to exchange lists with their partners. Several pairs may conduct the exercise simultaneously as they sit around the room. One member of each pair starts off by reading his partner's list. After reading each item, such as, "I am overweight," the person reading the list goes on to describe how *he* would feel if this quality applied to him. He goes on, drawing upon his own experiences, and speaks for a minute or so about the inferences he can make regarding the item on the list—advantages, disadvantages, implications.

The partner whose list is being read is to listen but make no reply until after both have finished the exercise. When one finishes reading and commenting on his partner's list, the other does likewise. The exercise should take about twenty minutes. Only after both partners have read the other's list should they give feedback and engage in a discussion. It is unimportant whether or not the participants are correct; what is essential is the willingness to make intuitive inferences based on the qualities noted on the lists.

A similar exercise for a small group is "secret pooling." Each group member writes a "secret" on a piece of paper. The secret should be about something which he personally would feel quite uncomfortable revealing to the group. The papers are all folded in the same fashion, and mixed thoroughly with those of the others in the group to ensure anonymity. When the papers are redistributed each one checks quickly to make sure the paper he picked is not his own. Then, in turn, each person reads out the secret he picked as if it were *his own secret*. He speaks in the first person, and goes on to explain (making inferences and taking risks of interpretation) how it feels to have that secret as part of one's own life history. He speaks for a minute or so, talking about the feelings and attitudes which are associated with the contents of the secret he reads. Then another group member reads the secret *he* picked.

It is often surprising and relieving to group members to find that others talk about their anonymously written secret with empathy and kindness; the commonness of themes is also usually striking in this exercise. Through the discovery of shared feelings about emotional issues, the group moves toward greater group cohesion. This exercise thus serves many functions in developing empathic skills as well as serving as a warm-up for further group activities.

A more playful exercise is the "directed-fantasy double." The director speaks to the group as follows: "Think of an object, animal, or character in fairytale—and then become that thing.

What is your future? Past? The more you do this, the more you will be ready to empathically move into a variety of roles.''

SUMMARY

In summary, the auxiliary ego and, in particular, the double, add the distinguishing characteristics of psychodramatic enactment to the field of action approaches in psychotherapy and education. In particular, the double role provides not only a powerful stimulus to the protagonist, but equally important offers an opportunity for building empathic skills in the person who doubles.

References

Deutsch, Felix. Analytic posturology and synesthesiology. *Psychoanalytic Revuew,* Spring 1963, *50,* 40-67.

Deutsch, Felix. Entering the mind through the sensory gateways in associative anamnesis. *Psychosomatic Medicine,* 1960, *22*(6), 466-480.

Ferreira, A. Empathy and the bridge function of the ego. *Journal of American Psychoanalytic Association,* 1961, *9*(1), 91-105.

Goldstein, S. Effects of doubling on involvement in group psychotherapy. *Psychotherapy: Theory, Research and Practice,* 1967, *4*(2), 57-60.

Katz, Robert L. *Empathy–Its nature and use.* New York: Free Press, 1963.

Krainen, James M. Counter-playing: A group therapy technique. *American Journal of Psychiatry,* 1972, *129* (5): 600-601.

Leveton, Eva. *Psychodrama for the timid clinician.* Palo Alto: Science and Behavior Books, 1973.

Moreno, Zerka Toeman. The auxiliary ego, double, and mirror techniques. *Sociometry,* 1946, *9,* 178.

Moreno, Zerka T. The double situation in psychodrama. *Sociatry,* 1948, *1*(4), 436-448.

Ossorio, A. and Fine, Leon. Psychodrama as a catalyst for social change in a mental hospital, in J. Masserman and J. L. Moreno (Eds.) *Reviews and integrations,* Volume 5 of *Progress in psychotherapy.* New York: Grune and Stratton, 1960.

Toeman, Zerka. See Moreno, Zerka Toeman.

Walstedt, Joyce. Teaching empathy. *Mental Hygiene,* 1968, *52*(4), 600-611.

4

The Warm-up

The *warm-up,* in its more restricted sense, refers to the first phase of a psychodramatic enactment in which a protagonist is helped to become involved enough to move into action. In a broader sense, *warming up* is an important psychological phenomenon which is all too often neglected. To *warm up* to any activity requires the *gradual* increase of physical movement, the inclusion of *spontaneous behaviors,* and the *direction of attention* toward some specific idea or task. The principles of warming up apply not only to structuring the first stage of any psychodramatic involvement, but also to many areas of everyday life. This chapter will focus primarily on the practical aspects of using warming-up techniques in psychodrama.

The most important issue in warming up is the establishment of a context which fosters *spontaneity.* The necessary conditions for spontaneous behavior include (1) a sense of trust and safety; (2) norms which allow for the inclusion of nonrational and intuitive dimensions; (3) some feeling of tentative distance, which is one element of "playfulness"; and (4) a movement toward risk-taking and exploration into novelty. The theory of spontaneity has been written about at length by Dr. Moreno and others, and supplemental reading in these and related articles is recommended.

The first phase of any group activity involves the development of some concensus as to the purposes, methods, duration, dimensions, and division of responsibilities in the group. The group leader may identify himself and facilitate introductions. Some talking by the group leader, whom we will now call the director, often starts the group toward clarification of the task.

THE DIRECTOR'S WARM-UP

The director is best able to function in the use of psychodramatic methods only if he himself is warmed up. To achieve this he should be physically active in walking about, moving chairs, talking with the group about a variety of topics, presenting a basic introduction regarding what he will be doing, how long the group will last, etc. All these activities build a dynamic and imaginative warm-up in himself. (Few things are more counter-productive to a group's warming up than a director who talks with the group from a sitting position; see Figure 4)

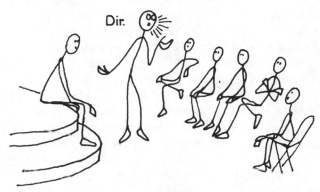

Figure 4

During his own warm-up, the director is developing spontaneity in himself. This is his way of disclosing some of his own style. If he can communicate a sense of authenticity and warmth, his warming up begins to allow the group to know and trust him. His behavior further models for the group the norms of self-disclosure, spontaneity, acceptance of humor, toleration of some distance (i.e., the acceptability of some reserve on the part of the group members and a respect for some unwillingness to engage in significant self-disclosure at first), and the acceptability of action and forceful expression. The director is meanwhile interacting with the group, and developing a level of *tele* with them. (*Tele* is Moreno's term for a multileveled, multidirectional sense of relationship: a term richer than *rapport* and more mutual than *transference and counter-transference*.)

Of course, during this first phase the director is also mentally warming up to the task that lies ahead. He must be able to assess the many factors which could affect the group process: a skill that comes only with much reading and experience (see Chapter 10). The director must also become aware of his own resistances to the group, if any are present.

A common way in which a director might experience resistance to the group lies in his own lack of preparation or in the presence of any artificial expectations he may have. Does the director feel he must "put on a show"? Does he have stereotyped attitudes towards some of the group members? Does he wish he could avoid dealing with the group's stereotypes of himself?

The director may cope with these mixed feelings and expectations of himself using several techniques, all of which facilitate his own warming up: (1) he may discuss his plans and apprehensions in advance with a co-worker; (2) he may review his own tolerance for not needing a "dramatic happening" to occur as part of his introduction to the group, thus clarifying his own position at the outset; (3) he may allow his own *negative tele* to be first on the agenda for the group discussion or psychodrama; or (4) if he feels a great deal of over-involvement, he should decline to direct, and if another potential director is available, that person should be allowed to take over the leadership role.

GROUP COHESION

In the next phase, following the basic self-introduction and his own warm-up, the director helps to develop group cohesion. The first step in building a sense of group identity and trust is to get the group members to know each other. The director may choose to employ a variety of introductory exercises. He can modify these exercises to meet the purposes of the group task:

The director asks each member to find a partner to get to know him. Then, in a few minutes he asks each of the group members to introduce his partner to the group. Partners may be chosen as people one knows, strangers, someone who seems very different from oneself, someone with whom one has felt some conflict, or one's spouse. A series of these *dyads* may be structured in order to have each group member not only meet, but experience something different with each partner, thus consolidating the partner's name in his memory. Some nonverbal exercises can be included in these dyads: "talking" with hands or backs, trust walks, and so forth. (In the *trust walk* or *blind walk,* one partner takes the blindfolded other on a little tour, emphasizing the awareness of trust issues.)

By the use of *self-presentation,* each person is asked to introduce himself and to say something about his background, expectations, and the like.

The use of action exercises early in the group's development may blend into the use of other structured experiences which are designed not only as introductions, but also as steps in building trust, self-disclosure, and playfulness. They are also useful as an introduction to a variety of modalities, such as guided imagination and nonverbal communication.

GROUP TASK AND WARM-UP TECHNIQUES

The use of action exercises or structured experiences not only works toward the task of building group cohesion, but also serves to sensitize each group member to those dimensions of his personality with which he has the greatest conflict—his "blind spots." I find that about one-fifth of any group is unaffected by any given exercise; another fifth is quite affected: the technique really arouses an awareness of some conflict area; and the rest of the group is mildly affected. After several exercises, most of the group members become more aware of their own problems.

At this point, the director moves into developing a theme or finding a protagonist. If the group is warming up slowly, or the director would like to start at some distance, the discussion of some topic of general interest may come next. Some further techniques include:

In groups that already know each other, the director may simply wait in the background while the group warms itself up, discussing and joking about a variety of topics. Often a common theme emerges after several minutes, which the director may capitalize on by turning it into an enactment. This approach is called the *undirected warm-up*.

If the group knows its own task, the director simply starts with a discussion, or uses a concrete example with which to explore sociodramatically some of the issues. This would be called a *directed warm-up*.

After the group has developed some group cohesion, the director discusses the group theme at a distance, using situations which are somewhat removed from real life. Some of these warm-ups include:

The melodrama   A group member could possibly be the director. The members could then have "auditions" for the various parts: heroine, hero, villain, heroine's mother, father, or others; the basic plot is that the mortgage is to be foreclosed unless the heroine gives herself to the villain; the sawmill or railroad tracks scenes follow; then the rescue. Improvisations and "hamming it up" are encouraged. Fairy tales and myths can also be enacted.

Situation tests   For individuals or groups. Examples include: the "lifeboat"—who will be chosen to die?; "left on a desert island"—how will the group organize itself?; "the stranger in the town restaurant"; "the pick-up"; "the employment interview"; and so on. A range of dramatic, fantasied, humorous, tragic, or frustrating situations, from slight to extreme, can be used.

The magic shop   This is an especially useful technique. The director has the group imagine a small shop on the stage. The shopkeeper may be played by a trained auxiliary, a member of the group, or even by the director himself. The group is told that on the shelves of this magic shop all manner of wonderful qualities can be found. Anyone who wishes to buy may come into the shop. Eventually someone volunteers to become the customer-protagonist.

When the customer first asks for his heart's desire, his opening requests are often quite vague: I want "love," "wisdom," "immortality," "success," etc. As the first task, the shopkeeper engages the customer in a discussion in order to clarify more specifically what he wants, e. g., from whom does he want love? What conditions will he accept? This conversation should remain within the metaphor of a shopkeeper simply trying to understand what is desired. The more general the desire, the more expensive or inexpensive it may be: "You want love from *everybody?* Well, that will cost quite a bit more," says the shopkeeper.

The negotiation of the price comprises the second task within the technique of the magic shop. Money cannot be offered, The shopkeeper explains that he can only accept in barter some quality or facet of the customer's life or personality which he would be willing to sacrifice—something that someone *else* might wish to buy some day from the magic shop. The price offered often leads to some thought-provoking challenges:

Customer: I'll give up my selfishness for love!
Shopkeeper: Are you willing to give up *all* of your selfishness?
Customer: Well, now . . .

The director may allow either the protagonist or the auxiliary-shopkeeper to consult with the audience for their advice. What would be a fair price for immortality?

Often a customer will claim an inability to think of something to offer as his payment. (The statement, "I don't know," betrays a passive-dependent stance and should be redefined as, "I'm having difficulty thinking of something.") This situation not only demonstrates the protagonist's passive style, but also can be a starting point from which to explore the protagonist's lack of awareness of his inner resources.

Once the tentative bargain has been struck, the protagonist is encouraged to try out his newly purchased qualities, or to see how he gets along without the quality he has just given up. In these follow-up symbolic enactments, the protagonist may find that he has a greater need than he believed for what he was ready to give up; or, on the other hand, that what he thought he wanted was not all what he expected. For example, the man who wanted an agreeable wife found that he was bored by the enactment of his "ideal" mate. The girl who would give up "being controlling" felt too vulnerable when she had to enact a situation blindfolded.

In summary, the magic shop is an excellent technique not only for warming-up a group, but also for the purposes of clarifying goals and examining the consequences of one's choices.

Guided fantasy refers to a wide variety of exercises in which the director has the group members imagine a variety of general themes, the details of which are filled in by each individual's unique imagery. Picturing trips through one's own body, journeys through forests, mountains, houses, or into the sea—are all common themes. This technique has also been called the *directed daydream* method, and has become a major approach within the general school of *psychosynthesis*. The group can utilize these methods individually, while working in dyads, or they can share a fantasy together as a group. The works of Leuner, Assagioli, Desoille, and Gerard are all receiving increasing recognition in this area.

Another major group of warm-ups are those derived from the related fields of the arts as adjunctive therapies.

Theater games and exercises from the mime can be adapted as warm-ups for psychodramatic enactments. Activities derived from creative dramatics are widely utilized in school settings, and can easily lead to explorations of more meaningful issues.

Dance and all the exercises which lead to spontaneity and involvement in expressiveness can easily be part of any warm-up. Related to the field of dance are the activities derived from body movement, sensory awakening, bioenergetics, and rhythmical group rituals. Simple voiced intonations—chants, grunts, repetitive noises—can all be added to emphasize breathing and expressive action. These warm-ups not only generate a great deal of readiness for action, but also establish a norm of physical involvement within the group.

Music can be used in a variety of ways. The group members can create and/or play simple instruments in an improvisatory style. The interplay can be heightened by a mixture of making music, voice sounds, and body movement. The introduction of simple musical instruments, elementary circle dance, and stretching activities is expecially valuable in working with patients who have been passive or institutionalized for long periods.

Background music may also be an effective catalyst to group interaction. The lyrics of many contemporary songs can suggest common emotional themes for group discussion. A trained music therapist can use his flexible ability to provide different moods in music which will accompany and heighten the flow of action in many enactments

Artistic materials can be adapted to a group setting. Paints, clay, papier-mâché, pastels, crayons, finger paints, colored sand, and a wide variety of collage materials are all useful in this regard. Starting with ideas derived from art therapy, the group can move from the creative media to enactments and then back to further involvement in artistic creation.

One example of the use of artistic materials is *shared drawings:* in a couples group, each pair is asked to create a picture together, without using any words; the drawing is to represent their relationship. About fifteen minutes are allotted for this, and then the director has each couple in turn display and discuss its picture.

All of the above-mentioned approaches can become warm-up techniques that emphasize spontancity and a validation of the creative dimensions within the self.

Finally, each director will undoubtedly improvise a variety of modifications of any of the above-mentioned techniques. James Sacks, for example, combines elements of many different approaches in one of his warm-ups: The group members form a fairly tight circle, sitting on cushions or low seats. The director asks them to lean forward; each member is then to state his name (or nickname) and to mention what he hopes to achieve in the group session. *All* of these statements are to be no greater than one sentence in length. Other directions follow: "Share with the group something they don't know about you; tell an old, old memory; name someone with whom you have unfinished business." At this point, the one-sentence rule may be lifted. The group members are then asked to dictate a letter to the person with whom they have unfinished business. This technique is likely to be useful in building group cohesion, encouraging self-disclosure, and developing themes and protagonists for future enactments.

THE SELECTION OF A PROTAGONIST

There are several ways in which a protagonist may emerge out of the group process:

The protagonist may volunteer in that or an earlier session. The director may want to have the group vote on whom is to be dealt with if there are several volunteers, or he may arbitrarily choose in what order they will be protagonists.

The director may simply wait quietly until someone does volunteer, but the director has to know where to use this approach or it may backfire. Some groups will simply not respond.

The protagonist may be preselected by the therapists.

The director may walk around and converse with different people in the group until he finds someone who is ready to be the protagonist; or he may try a common warm-up, such as the "auxiliary chair," and see who emerges as the most likely candidate.

Figure 5

The protagonist may emerge out of the natural ongoing group process. This occurs when the group arrives and is catalyzed into some natural joking or discussion of a topic. This spontaneity should not be suppressed by an unspoken or explicit "let's get down to business," which has the effect of a wet blanket on a fire. People do not like to talk about their problems: it is humiliating, and such a suggestion invariably quenches spontaneity in a group. Instead, the director should wait. He may even go along with the joking, trusting that he can gently turn it into a meaningful issue. Eventually both a theme and a protagonist emerge.

The director, especially in work or school situations, may start with a short talk on some general theme. If it is controversial, so much the better. The group may find itself agreeing or disagreeing, and this can then be made explicit by setting up a spectogram (see p. 99).

Using spectograms, sociodramas, or other group-centered methods, a protagonist may emerge as one who is especially concerned about something triggered in the discussion. In addition, in order to stimulate a protagonist, or to help him become more involved in his life situation, the director can use more individual-centered warm-ups:

The auxiliary chair   This is a major warm-up method and can also be used at times during the action session. The director puts forward an empty chair and says, "There is someone sitting in this chair—someone important to you. Visualize him or her, what he is doing, wearing, what he might be thinking about, etc. . . When he's clear to you, raise a finger." Then when most have indicated they have seen someone, the director may proceed to ask whom they see in the chair. The director may ask no one in particular and wait for volunteers, or address his question to a specific person. When someone responds, he is either asked to be that person (and sit in the chair) or is asked what he has to say to whomever he sees in the chair. This can lead to a brief interchange which may lead to a further enactment.

During an enactment, the auxiliary chair can also be used when the protagonist has difficulty relating to a real person. The chair in this sense becomes the major instrument in monodrama. (See Figure 2, p. 19.)

*The action sociogram** In this method, the protagonist presents his "social atom"—the key people most relevant to his experience (often his family) as if they were a group of sculptures in a diorama, or a three-dimensional painting (see Figure 6). Members of the group become auxiliary egos and portray these significant figures. With the help of the director, the protagonist positions them in characteristic poses which symbolically portray their essential relationship to the protagonist (who is also portrayed within the scene by an auxiliary). The use of the posture, the direction in which each figure faces, and the proximity or distance from the protagonist in the scene may all symbolically represent the quality of the relationship. Finally, the protagonist gives each figure in the scene a characteristic sentence or phrase to speak, which symbolically brings them "to life." He then steps back and observes, or enters the scene and begins to relate to his family or central group.

Figure 6

Another variant of the action sociogram is for the director to use physical objects to represent the social atom: a group of coins of various denominations; a chess set; or a set of hand

*Dr. Moreno wishes it noted that he was the originator of the basic work on the action sociogram.

puppets (preferably of animals). The protagonist is instructed to identify the chessman or hand puppet of his choice with one of the people in his social atom. It is often interesting for example, to watch a protagonist pick the mouse hand puppet, or the pawn for the father; the bear puppet, or bishop for the brother, etc. Which figure, where it is placed, and what it does can then lead to an extrapolation from the symbolic situation to the dynamics of the protagonist's social atom.

MOVING INTO ACTION

After the protagonist has emerged from the group the last phase of the warm-up remains. The basic issue is discussed with the protagonist as he emerges at eye level in the group. "Yes, that issue troubles me," is the essence of the contract. "Let's work on it," says the director, and the protagonist is led gently by the hand to the center of the group.

Depending on his readiness, the protagonist may sit at the second level-edge of the stage or on a chair in the staging area, and the director sits with him (Figure 7). The director discusses the issue further, asking him what the nature of the issue is. He waits for just enough answers to arrive at a specific example: a place or a person. Then, the enactment quickly moves to the third level.

Figure 7

The director takes an appropriate cue that points to an enactment and suggests it. If a name of someone who seems important to the protagonist is mentioned, possibly an interaction with that person is to be the "first scene." If a time of life is mentioned, the director moves toward a specific memory or image.

During the warm-up, the protagonist is encouraged to gradually move upwards and centrally in the room, and is helped to engage in increasing activity. When a protagonist is warmed up to an unusually high pitch he will almost direct the drama by himself.

If, during the warm-up, the protagonist shows increasing anxiety which is manifested by resistance, the director must shift the enactment into a less emotionally loaded sphere of exploration while still continuing the action. This is similar to the process of desensitization by imagery and relaxation in the treatment of phobic patients: If the client indicates that he is picturing a scene which makes him too tense, the therapist allows him to return to a less frightening image with which he can relax, but the therapy continues. Similarly, if the protagonist "freezes," the director may ask him to soliloquize, or to use one of the following warm-ups:

Hand puppets   A puppet show can often be an effective warm-up, while giving the protagonist some distance. The use of masks may have a similar function.

Blackout   The entire theater is blacked out although all actions continue as if there would be full daylight. This is done so that the protagonist may go through a painful experience unobserved, and so the protagonist can retain the experience of solitude.

Turn your back   A protagonist is occasionally embarrassed to present a particular episode while facing the group. He is then permitted to turn his back to the group and to act as if he were alone, in his own home, or wherever the episode takes place. Once the protagonist has reached a sufficient degree of involvement, he is then ready to carry on in facing the audience.

Portrayal of a dream   is often an excellent first enactment for a protagonist's exploration of his problem. This is often done in Gestalt therapy.

Hypnodrama   The protagonist is hypnotized and then helped to enact his situation in a hypnotic state.

At this point, the protagonist is usually ready to enter the second phase of the psychodrama—*the action,* which will be discussed in the next chapter.

SUMMARY

The warming up process is the first and essential part of any enactment and is based on the fundamental need for any person to *gradually* develop increasing involvement and spontaneity through goal-directed physical action. In reference to group process, the warm-up phase applies to the components of (1) the director's warm-up, (2) building group cohesion, (3) developing a group theme, (4) finding a protagonist, and (5) moving the protagonist onto the stage.

References

Bringham, F. M. Masks as a psychotherapeutic modality. *Journal of American Osteopathic Association,* February, 1970, *69,* 549-555.

Chace, Marian. Rhythm and movement as used in St. Elizabeth's Hospital. *Sociometry,* 1945, *8,* 481-483.

Corynetz, Paul. The warming-up process of an audience. *Sociometry,* 1945, *8*(3-4), 218-225.

Enneis, James M. The dynamics of group and action processes in therapy. *Group Psychotherapy,* 1951, *4*(1), 17-21.

Enneis, James M. The hypnodramatic technique. *Group Psychotherapy,* 1950, *3*(1), 11-40.

Fielding, Benjamin. Enactment of dreams in group psychotherapy. *Psychotherapy: Theory, Research and Practice,* 1967, *4*(2), 74.

Fine, Leon J. Nonverbal aspects of psychodrama, in J. Masserman and J. L. Moreno (Eds.) *Social psychotherapy,* Volume 4 of *Progress in psychotherapy.* New York: Grune and Stratton, 1959.

Galper, Jeffry. Nonverbal communication exercises in groups. *Social Work,* 1970, *15*(2), 68-71.

Gendzel, Ivan B. Marathon group therapy and nonverbal methods. *American Journal of Psychiatry,* 1970, *127*(3), 286-290.

Hammer, Max. The directed daydream technique. *Psychotherapy: Theory, Research and Practice,* 1967, *4*(4), 173.

Kipper, D. A. On spontaneity. *Group Psychotherapy,* 1967, *20*(1).

Kole, Delbert. The spectrogram in psychodrama. *Group Psychotherapy,* 1967, *20*(1-2), 53-61.

Kors, Pieter C. Unstructured puppet shows as group procedures in therapy with children. *Psychiatric Quarterly Supplement*, 1964, *38*(1), 56-75.

Leuner, Hans Carl. Guided affective imagery. *American Journal of Psychotherapy*, 1969, *23*(1), 4-22. Excellent basic article related to very important approach to psychotherapy. Amazingly effective technique to mobilize imagination.

Lippitt, Rosemary. Auxiliary chair technique. *Group Psychotherapy*, 1958, *11*(1-2), 8-23.

Malamud, Daniel I. and Machover, Solomon. *Toward self-understanding: Group techniques for self-confrontation*. Springfield, Ill.: Charles C Thomas, 1965. Very good book on workshops for students learning interpersonal sensitivity. He offers a wide variety of methods and many ideas on how to run a workshop or class.

Middleman, Ruth R. *The nonverbal method in working with groups*. New York: Associated Press, 1968.

Mintz, Elizabeth. Therapy techniques and encounter techniques. *American Journal of Psychotherapy*, 1971, *25*(1), 107.

Moreno, Jacob L. Hypnodrama and psychodrama. *Group Psychotherapy*, 1950, *3*(1), 1-10.

Moreno, Zerka T. A survey of psychodramatic techniques. *ACTA Psychotherapeutica*, 1959, *7*, 197-206.

Otto, H. A. *Group methods to actualize human potential: A handbook*. Beverly Hills: Holistic Press, 1970. Lists a variety of action methods, workshops—very interesting.

Pankratz, Lorne and Buchan, Gerald. Exploring psychodrama techniques with defective delinquents. *Group Psychotherapy*, 1965, *18*(3), 136-141.

Pfeiffer, J. W. and Jones, J. E. *Structured experience for human relations training*. Iowa City: University Associates Press, 1969, 3 vols.

Sacks, James M. The judgment technique. *Group Psychotherapy*, 1966, *19*(29), 29-31.

Sacks, James M. Psychodrama, the warm-up. *Group Psychotherapy*, 1967, *20*(4), 118-121.

Seabourne, Barbara. The action sociogram. *Group Psychotherapy*, 1963, *16*(3), 145-155.

Seabourne, Barbara. Warm-up of protagonist and auxiliary egos. Unpublished paper, St. Louis State Hospital, 1966.

Spolin, Viola. *Improvisations for the theater*. Evanston, Ill.: Northwestern University Press, 1963. Theater games can be modified to become warm-ups in psychodrama.

Stevens, John A. *Awareness: Exploring, experimenting, experiencing*. Lafayette, Cal.: Real People Press, 1971. Excellent book on many exercises.

Streitfeld, H. S. and Lewis, Howard R. *Growth games*. New York: Harcourt, Brace, Jovanovich, 1971.

Warner, G. Douglas. The didactic auxiliary chair. *Group Psychotherapy,* 1970, *23* (1-2), 31-34.

Weiner, Hannah A. and Sacks, James M. Warm-up and sum-up. *Group Psychotherapy,* 1969, *22*(1-2), 85-102. Many useful techniques and ideas.

Yablonsky, Lewis and Enneis, James. M. Psychodrama, theory and practice, in Frieda Fromm-Reichman and J. L. Moreno (Eds.) *Progress in psychotherapy,* Vol. 1. New York: Grune and Stratton, 1956.

Zweben, Joan and Hamman, K. Prescribed games: A theoretical perspective on the use of group techniques. *Psychotherapy: Theory, Research and Practice,* 1970, *7*(1), 22-27.

5

The Action

This chapter will discuss the process of the second phase of the psychodrama, the *action* portion. Following the warm-up of the group and the selection of the protagonist, the director is then faced with the challenge of staging the enactment in order to most fully help the protagonist portray the psychological dimensions of his problem.

It should be noted that every psychodramatic enactment is unique—there is no fixed sequence of events. In general, however, there is a movement toward the core conflict and greater emotional expression as the drama unfolds. The different phases in the enactment vary in each case, but usually follow the order of presentation in this chapter.

PRESENTATION OF THE PROBLEM

When the protagonist is selected, he is brought toward the stage and is encouraged to describe his situation. As the director discusses the protagonist's problem a specific example is sought. Then if the protagonist begins to narrate the situation, the director encourages him to *portray* the scene, rather than to *talk about* what happened (Figure 7, p. 47).

Protagonist ("Joe"): Well, I had this fight with my boss . . .

Director: Show us, don't tell us. (The director gets up and gently holds Joe's arm as he moves into the stage area:) Where does the scene happen? (Figure 8)

Joe: It was in the office.

Figure 8

Director: It *is* in the office— it's happening *now!* Let's see the office . . . where is the boss's chair? . . . desk? . . . Are you sitting or standing? (Figure 9)

Figure 9

The director continues to speak in the present tense, reinforcing the protagonist's immersion in the here-and-now.

The protagonist is helped to move around the stage, visualizing the scene. The invitation to act in the here-and-now has an almost hypnotic effect: it is surprising how easily and naturally most protagonists become involved in the scene.

As the protagonist describes the scene, the director asks him to point out the furniture and comment on the textures of the materials, the colors, the weather—all concrete sensations which immerse him even more deeply in the enactment. The setting of the stage is for the protagonist's benefit, not the audience's. It may be as brief or prolonged as the director feels is necessary in order to maximize the protagonist's continuing warm-up. He is instructed to move around the stage, positioning the chairs himself. Encouragement of the protagonist's physical action in walking and moving further increases his warm-up. It is important to maximize physical activity throughout the psychodramatic

Figure 10

enactment in order to avoid becoming bogged down in a wordy
interaction (one of the most common pitfalls of directing). Later
in the psychodrama, the director continues to use a variety of
scene changes, role reversals, standing on chairs, pushing, climb-
ing over furniture, and many other techniques in order to keep
up the pace of action.

BRINGING IN THE AUXILIARY

As the scene is set, the auxiliary egos are chosen and encouraged to move immediately into their roles.

Director: Okay, let's have someone to play your boss (Figure
10).

Joe is asked to pick someone in the group—(call him Bill) to
be the auxiliary. Bill comes on stage and the director immediately
warms him up to his role:

Director: Mr. Jones, you asked Joe to come in today . . . he
can't hear you right now . . . if you were just thinking out loud

Figure 11

to yourself, giving a "soliloquy," let's hear what you have to say regarding why you want to see him.

Auxilary Ego (Bill, as Mr. Jones): Well, Joe hasn't been performing very well at his job (Figure 11).

Director (glancing at Joe): Is that right?

Joe: No, that's not it . . . my work is fine.

Director: Change parts (role-reverse) . . . Joe, be Mr. Jones and begin the encounter.

Joe (as Mr. Jones): Look, Joe, this is the third time this week you've come in late.

Director: Change parts and start again . . . Mr. Jones (Aside murmuring): Repeat the last line.

A. E. (Mr. Jones): Look Joe, this is, etc. . . (Figure 12).

Figure 12

Joe: But, Sir, when I took this job we agreed that because of my having to take care of my kids my work time would be adjusted!

A. E. Well, the other employees are noticing and complaining . . .

The issues are unfolding. If the auxiliary ego does not play his part as the protagonist visualizes its essential quality, further role-reversals are used to guide the auxiliary ego towards a more accurate role portrayal.

If the protagonist tends to narrate to the audience, the auxiliary should address him "in-role."

A. E. You're talking as if I'm not even here! What's the big idea of being so late this morning!

If the protagonist becomes lost in intellectualizations or confused as to his feelings, there are some other techniques which may be used:

The protagonist can enact the scene without using words, using sounds without words ("blah-blah" or gibberish) or no sounds at all, simply gestures. The former induces the protagonist to increase the pace, tone rhythm, and inflections of his voice, which exaggerates the expression of feeling without content. The latter, using no sounds at all, channels him toward dramatizing his gestures and expressions, which also throws the emotional components of the interaction into sharp contrast.

Soliloquy The protagonist is instructed to walk up and down and talk to himself out loud, in order to clarify his feelings. He can then re-enter the interaction with the auxiliary ego (Mr. Jones).

If the protagonist has difficulty expressing his emotions clearly,

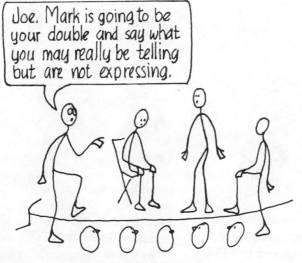

Figure 13

a *double* may be brought in: an auxiliary who will be Joe's inner feelings (See Figure 13 and also Chapter 3).

Director: Mark, will you come in here. (Gives instructions for doubling, then carries on with the scene.)

Joe (continuing): Well, Sir, I think that isn't what we agreed on . . .

Mr. Jones: Look Joe, we have to run a business here . . .

Double: Look, you bastard . . .

Joe (nodding): Yeah! You can't push me around like this!

Mr. Jones: Well! I never. . . !

Double: It's about time someone was frank with you! When you make an agreement . . . (Figure 14).

Figure 14

Joe:—Yeah, you have to stand by what you say!

From this point, the interaction can be continued, replayed, or the scene shifted and a related interaction portrayed. If Joe has problems with authority, many other encounters with authority figures can be explored, always moving to more central emotional issues.

MOVING FROM PERIPHERAL TO CENTRAL

Often the protagonist is warmed up enough to begin an enact-ment, but the "core" conflict is still buried under explanations and descriptions of circumstances. This "resistance" is not only to be allowed, but actually *used* in building a preliminary scene. The director should respect the protagonist's need to start at the periphery of a problem.

For example, if the protagonist has difficulty in dealing with an emotionally-loaded conflict with his mother, he may be helped to enact a similar situation with a saleslady. Another technique is to have the protagonist play the role of his own brother or sister, and to interact with his mother from that position. Marguerite Parrish wrote about the following two useful techniques:

The substitute role technique is frequently used and is helpful when working with protagonists who tend to be suspicious and resist portraying themselves on the stage. This technique was successfully used with a middle aged woman diagnosed as having involutional melancholia with some paranoid traits. She was unable to enact her own situations and so was asked to play the role of her mother, who operated a boarding-house. In this role she was at ease and seemed to enjoy going on the stage. During the third session the protagonist brought up the fact that one of her roomers was promiscuous. This story was also her own story. As a young girl her illegitimate pregnancy was followed by an abortion, and as she approached middle life she worried about this incident and felt sure her family would find out and would no longer love her. Psychodrama gave this woman an opportunity to freely express her feelings about the incident, and the discussion of the audience helped her to see that she had the love of her family and would not necessarily lose it because of that past event.

In the *symbolic distance technique* the protagonist enacts a role very different from his own role and is gradually led to portray his own role. This technique is particularly valuable when working with children. A young boy and girl from broken and inadequate homes were treated in this way. Individual therapy was helpful and outward behavior improved, but the children were afraid to leave the security of the hospital, for they felt sure they could not get along in a home situation. Because the problems of these children were so alike, they were cast as brother and sister and were treated together. Following the portrayals, the group discussed why the children acted differently in the various situations. From these scenes the children finally came to realize that they could get along in some types of family homes and expressed willingness to accept a family care situation.

If the protagonist tends to speak in terms of abstractions, these concepts can be made concrete by symbolizing them as figures with their own personalities: "They; "Society"; "other people"; "the establishment"; "young people"; all can be portrayed by an auxiliary ego. "This man *is* the Establishment. Talk to him now." The protagonist is directed to confront the auxiliary and eventually role-reverse with him, all of which brings the protagonist's conflicts into sharper focus.

FOCUSING ON THE NONVERBAL

One of the most useful approaches in clarifying the protagonist's problem is the emphasis on explicitly portraying the nonverbal communications involved, e. g.:

Joe (protagonist): But Sir, you *said* you would.

Director: Joe, step out of the scene. Mark, replay that interaction, acting the exact way Joe behaves)*mirror technique*.)

Mark (Auxiliary ego, whining as in Figure 15.) "But Sir, etc. . . .

Joe: Wow! Do I whine like that?

Dir: (to the group): Is Mark's presentation fair? (Group agrees). Well, Joe . . . with whom did you "whine" as a child? . . .

Joe: To my father . . . when he, etc.

Often what is said in an interaction (the content) is less important than *how* it is said (the process). The dramatization of the expression, posture, tone of voice, angle of the body, and gesture, all help bring out the factors which may have been the major determinants of the other person's reaction.

Role reversal, observations from the audience, and the amplifi-

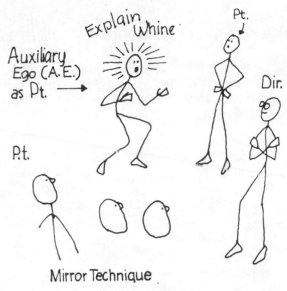

Mirror Technique

Figure 15

cation of gesture, as well as the mirror technique, help the protagonist and group become more aware of the nature and importance of the nonverbal communication being portrayed in the
interaction.

EXPLORING UNEXPRESSED EMOTIONS

In psychodrama the protagonist presents not only what happened in reality, but more importantly, what may never have
actually occurred except in his own fantasy. One main importance
of psychodrama is that it brings onto the stage the protagonist's
hopes, fears, expectations, unexpressed resentments, projections,
internalizations, and judgmental attitudes. Furthermore, the protagonist is helped to ventilate these feelings and symbolically
live through them.

In the case of the example being used in this chapter, Joe's
muted conversation with the boss is converted into an emotional
confrontation with the help of the expressive double.

As the scenes are changed to deal with other authority conflicts, a variety of techniques can be used to intensify the expression of feelings.

In dealing with a parent figure, the auxiliary ego as parent stands on a chair, so that Joe feels at a disadvantage. Conversely, Joe may stand on the chair in order to equalize the status and encourage self-assertion (Figure 16).

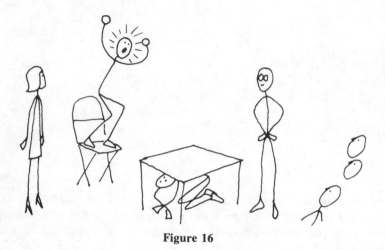

Figure 16

Colored lights, physical pushing or patronizing "head patting," and increasingly volatile counter-confrontation from the auxiliary can help the protagonist to express the many dimensions of his mixed feelings. In most psychodramas about an authority conflict, not only resentment toward authority is provoked; the need for "a good father" is also tapped.

Moreno calls psychodrama "the theater of truth" because what is enacted is, for the protagonist, the most important truth—the range of his own psychological realities.

MOVING WITH THE RESISTANCES

One major challenge of psychotherapy or psychodrama is that of helping the protagonist find a way to examine those inner feelings which are threatening to his sense of mastery or self-esteem. He may employ a wide range of resistances in order to avoid facing these unpleasant experiences. I find that if the director works *with* the resistances, there can often be a way found to gradually explore the deeper conflicts. Dr. Moreno puts it this way: "We don't tear down the protagonist's walls; rather, we simply try some of the handles on the many doors, and see which one opens."

The first step in dealing with a protagonist's resistances is the clear identification and expression of the *manner* in which he is avoiding a situation.

For example, Joe stands transfixed as he begins to think about his father.

Double: This is very hard for me. I'm not sure I want to talk about this.

Joe: Yes, I feel very tense. . . . The director then has the opportunity to support Joe in his fear.

Director: Being honest with someone so close is difficult—here, in psychodrama, we can face the challenge and it involves taking a risk, but it won't be overwhelming.

The second step in dealing with the resistance is that of exaggerating in the use of the defense. The resistance expressed in the tendency to "explain" may be portrayed openly by the director's asking the protagonist to talk to the group, to *explain* his position for one minute.

The protagonist's statement, "I can't seem to . . ." may be agreed with, but subtly re-defined by the double or the director as, "I won't. . . .

"I don't know," can be reshaped as, "I don't want to think about that. . . ."

"Why do I have to do this?" can be restated as, "I don't like doing this. . . ."

"It's no use," may be supported, with the addition of the temporary nature of the present resistance, *"Right now* I see no way out. . . ."

The point of going *with* the resistances is that through the explicit portrayal of the defenses, the protagonist becomes more fully aware that he is *choosing* to use a defense, i.e., it increases his awareness of his own responsibility for his behavior and sense of mastery over his habitual behavior patterns. The more a protagonist can allow himself, with the support of the director, to say "no," the sooner he begins to feel free to say "yes" when he is ready.

With a protagonist who is becoming overly anxious while dealing with a problem it is often appropriate to allow him to move away from the core conflict, to obtain some "distance." The move from peripheral issues toward central issues described earlier can be temporarily reversed.

Barbara Seabourne notes a variety of approaches which are helpful in dealing with difficult protagonists, e. g., the use of pleasant scenes, participation in many different stage experiences, the use of an opportunity to have an individual talking session with the director before the session, and so forth.

A major block in many protagonists is use of the defense mechanism of isolation of affect—they are not even aware that they *are* feeling. The first step in dealing with this resistance is to help the protagonist become aware of the experience of emotion within himself. Secondly, only when he is moved toward an attempt to identify the *quality* of the feeling, can he go on to explore the *meaning* of his emotions.

In dealing with sensitizing a protagonist to his own feelings, the director focuses on the protagonist's *nonverbal communications* and his *imagery*. These two "avenues to the unconscious" bypass the most common form of resistances: intellectualization, vagueness, explanation, rationalization, abstraction, and circumstantiality.

The protagonist's nonverbal communication is dramatized by treating the parts of the protagonist as if they were active beings in themselves: areas of tension in the body, tightness of the voice, gripping of the hands all can be enacted as a little encounter between different parts of the self, e. g.,:

Joe (to his "father"): Daddy, why don't you . . .
Director: Joe, what is your voice doing?
Joe: It's choked.
Director: Now become the part that's strangling the throat!
Joe (as throat): I'm being squeezed and strangled.

Director: Now become the part that's strangling the throat!
Joe (as strangler, rasping): Shut up you S. O. B. or you'll get us all into trouble! (as he twists his hands in a wringing motion).

This approach, like dream work, is used a great deal in Gestalt therapy and psychosynthesis.

The use of the *imagery* is a further avenue to the identification of deeper feelings. The different figures in a nightmare, hallucination, or a guided fantasy can interact using psychodramatic methods; and this can often clarify the nature of the protagonist's internal complexes, i.e., the conglomerations of attitudes, images, and emotions.

Dealing with a protagonist's resistances is the core of psychotherapy or psychodrama. The "art" of the director is tested nowhere more than in this task. This section of the chapter has only indicated some of the avenues of approach to a challenge which demands an individual response in each situation.

PRESENTING THE BASIC ATTITUDES

An important step in the psychodramatic exploration of a problem is the explicit portrayal of the protagonist's attitudes and basic assumptions about himself, others, and the nature of human relationships. These attitudes are often phrased in terms of internalized sentences, which start with "should" and "ought." Encouraging the protagonist to make these statements explicit is necessary because they represent the values of his superego.

Joe (soliloquizing on stage with his double): How could I hate my father? You're not supposed to hate your father!
Joe's Double: Right! I shouldn't hate him no matter what!
Joe: And anyway, I *love* him! How could I hate him?
Double: I can't love and hate at the same time!
Joe: Well, maybe I can . . .

Not only the protagonist's feelings are to be expressed, but also the attitudes which forbid the feelings from being accepted as part of his self-system. Some of these common attitudes include:

Men aren't supposed to cry
I should be able to handle this myself

Being emotional is a sign of weakness
If I start crying I may never stop
If I express my anger I'm afraid I might kill someone or lose control
If I try to love someone, he should be happy
If I'm not happy, it's because they don't *really* love me
One should be able to resolve his conflicts
I should have known this by now
If I haven't lived up to my expectations, I *must be* a failure

There are hundreds of such "internal commands." Many of these "lies we live by" can be found in the writings of Ronald Laing, Albert Ellis, A. H. Chapman, Walter O'Connell, and many others.

Another way to portray the different attitudes and complexes is to split the protagonist into different "selves," for example, one part might be the judging, rule-pronouncing complex, while the other part is the rebellious, or passive-aggressive, sulking self. (This is similar to Fritz Perls' concept of *top dog* vs. *underdog*, or Eric Berne's terminology of *Parent, Adult,* and *Child*.)

EXPLORING THE CORE CONFLICTS

The problem originally presented is often not at the root of the protagonist's emotional concerns. Basic attitudes have been established in earlier life, and it is the relationships of that period that are the next to be enacted. Sometimes what is indicated is not a movement from the present to the past, but from a relatively superficial to a more personal conflict, such as a sexual problem with a spouse or a struggle between different needs within the protagonist himself.

As these core relationships are portrayed, it may seem obvious to the director or the group that the protagonist is distorting the feelings of the other persons in his life. The director should be in no hurry to correct these distortions. First, the protagonist must present the situation as he experiences it: this is *his* "truth." He must experience being listened to. Only then does he become more receptive to exploring the possibility that the situation might have other points of view.

In our example of Joe, the director may explore scenes in which Joe wanted to be accepted by a father who had unrealistically high expectations of him. Joe's fantasies can be portrayed in scenes in which he is abandoned, rejected, or judged as inadequate by his father (Figure 17).

Figure 17

Joe role-reverses and portrays his own conception of his father's behavior. Indeed, Joe's portrayal of the father's judgment may be so harsh as to seem unrealistic to the audience: as if Joe is caricaturizing what a "bad father" does. This is probably because he is projecting onto his father the anger and guilt he feels within himself towards the weaknesses that only he himself secretly knows and condemns. Thus through role-reversal, the protagonist is helped to portray the distortions of his interpersonal perceptions by acting out what he believes others think (i.e., his own projections). This kind of approach can thus be an effective form of "diagnosis" of the protagonist's psychodynamics.

ACT HUNGER

Act hunger is the drive toward a fulfillment of the desires and impulses at the core of the self. The director should help the protagonist in a symbolic fulfillment of his act hunger. This is also a fundamental part of the protagonist's "psychological truth."

In the example of the enactment we have been using, the protagonist, Joe, finally confronts his father; he may gain some insight into the rage he has held toward his father by the director's helping him to portray his anger in *act fulfillment*. As the protagonist portrays the anger, themes of need and frustration, which are the bases of the anger, should be interwoven.

It is important that the director be aware of the psychotherapeutic maxim "Don't ventilate the hostility without the protagonist's also experiencing his dependency," that is to say, deal with the protagonist's *need* for something that is frustrated by the significant other. The catharsis of rage is usually a catharsis of longing.

For example, as Joe confronts his rigid, demanding father, whose unshakable coldness is dramatized and exaggerated by an auxiliary ego, Joe "escalates" his efforts to "get across to the old man," without any success. Finally, he is ready for violence; the director throws him a pillow and says, "There's your father—what do you feel like doing to him?"

Joe begins to beat the pillow, curse at the father, and, with the help of the double and director, express his pent up frustrations:

Joe: You never cared about *me!* All you saw was what *you* wanted! (He continues to strike the pillow, and is beginning to cry) You bastard! I wish you were dead! (Beats the pillow furiously and cries.) (See Figure 18).

At this point, after a full expression, the director may move in several directions. He may bring onto the stage an auxiliary to be the "good father" who can "see Joe for what he really is." The auxiliary may hold Joe and talk to him.

Figure 18

Another very powerful technique is the "death scene." It can be applied either to the death of the protagonist himself or as a vehicle to review the feelings in relationship to a significant other person.

In the first form, the protagonist is instructed to visualize his own death (the director may dim the lights). The director may warm up to the situation by asking him how he died, what it felt like, who is around him, and other related questions. The questions and final statements to others and (through role-reversal) of others towards the "dead" protagonist help clarify some of the emotional issues. (This method is useful for emphasizing the role of the "choosing, responsible self";—the "adult" ego state in transactional analysis terms.) Finally, the death scene can move towards a "rebirth scene."

The "death scene" may be interwoven with "judgment scenes," judgment of others, or of the self. The encounter with St. Peter is often a useful technique. (St. Peter is the archetypal figure who reviews the values and meaning of the protagonist's life with him.) St. Peter can play the role of the friendly and gentle interrogator. If the situation seems more appropriate for a judgment of the protagonist's life, members of the audience can be called in as jurors.

One variation of the death scene I like to use is the shift in St. Peter's role from "judge" to "philosopher." This usually

surprises people, for they are expecting St. Peter to be impressed
by status and "righteousness" issues, and upset by pecadilloes.
Instead, St. Peter simply asks: "How was it?" He does not
respond to answers of status, i.e., "what the protagonist proved."
Rather, he reiterates the focus on the issue of: "Did you do
what you had to do? Did you do it in your own way? Did you
'create' along the lines of your natural strengths, inclinations;
or did you fulfill your life in a role which was alien to your soul,
because you were trying to live up to someone else's expectations?"

Sometimes I follow this scene by giving the protagonist an
opportunity to enact the role he would choose if he could be
reborn in any kind of life he wanted.

A second major format of the death scene is more commonly
used, and involves the death of the significant other person. As
the protagonist seems involved in continuously struggling to
change the other person, to "make him see," the director may
stop and say, "He's dead now. . . ." or, "You have just received
a telegram notifying you of his death . . . you rush back and
stand at his bedside." Another variation is for the director to say
to the protagonist, "You have five minutes to talk to him before
he dies. Now is the time to make your goodbyes, ask your final
questions, express your honest resentments and appreciations."
For example:

Joe (to "dying father"): y'know Dad, I resented your judgment of me as a child. . . .

Director: Change parts. (Joe moves over and lays down, becoming the father)

Joe (as father): Well, son, I wanted so much for you . . . but
you've done okay (change parts)

Joe: Dad . . . how do you feel about me now? (change parts)

Father: Joe . . . I'm kinda proud of you . . . I really am. . . .

Joe: Dad . . . I love you, you know that?

A. E. (as father): I know son. (Joe weeps.)

Often the son makes his peace with his father in an atonement
(at-one-ment). "Saying goodbye" is an important method also
for reinforcing the protagonist's sense of identity. "I'm going on

. . . I don't need your support any longer . . . I can say goodbye
. . . It hurts, but I can let go."

Another powerful technique which can sometimes follow a
death-and-rebirth scene is "the crib scene." This method is also
useful in allowing the protagonist to experience his own dependency needs. The technique is often applied to the entire group,
including the protagonist. Doris Twitchell Allen describes it as
follows:

"Today we can he babies—just young infants in a crib. And
we can lie on the floor like babies , . pretend that you are a
baby."

Thus, the director gets one after another participant to lie on
the floor. After all are on the floor, lying as babies in a crib,
the psychodramatic director, in the role of the nurturing mother,
walks around from one to the other, patting them and covering
them with an imaginary blanket:

"So the baby goes to sleep, warm and quiet. So the baby gets
heavy, and goes to sleep . . . And the mother comes and loves
the baby. Takes care of the baby. Covers the baby and keeps
him warm. Feeds the baby and gives him milk. Pats the baby.
Watches over the baby and loves the baby. While the baby sleeps
and sleeps." (This is usually repeated several times during a five-
to-twenty minute sleep.)

The sleep period is followed by the waking-up period:

"So the baby begins to wake up. Begins to move a little,
stretches a little. Opens its eyes. Begins to sit up. Feels good,
feels alert, feels happy and content, sits up, gets up, gets back
in the chairs."

This is repeated as often as necessary for the group to wake
up, and finally ending with:

"Now as you sit back in your chairs you are adults again,
acting like adults. But for a while you were a baby and the mother
came and loved the baby and took care of the baby."

Back in the chairs, the patients discussed how they felt when
they were babies.

Of course, the above-mentioned techniques can be applied in
a multiplicity of situations, all depending on the sensitivity of
the director.

Act hunger involves more than the expressions of anger and dependency: the protagonist can gain important insights through fulfilling the desire to boast, perform, *demand* attention, express tenderness, dance, soar, hug, wrestle playfully, fall effortlessly, etc. Scenes of act completion can involve death and rebirth, risking and trusting.

Act completion has value in that it validates the protagonist's emotional experiences, thus reinforcing an integration of the previously rejected and suppressed dimensions of the personality—as some protagonists say after a catharsis, "It's OK for me to cry—it doesn't prove I'm weak," or, "Wow, I didn't know I had all that anger in me—I thought if I would start to let it out I'd never stop, but I guess I have more self-control than I thought." Thus, the protagonist can accept the anger, dependence, and other negatively valued emotions as part of himself and can re-define himself as one who, as a vital living being, contains many different feelings.

Act completion further validates the sense of *active choosing* as part of the self. There are many people who experience life as happening to them. They take a passive attitude, and feel themselves as rather lifeless and empty inside. The catharsis that so often accompanies the psychodramatic process represents an active taking into the *conscious* self all the different mixed feelings that had heretofore been rejected and suppressed. Along with the feelings of anger and yearning, there is a sense of "determination to go on," which becomes integrated into the protagonist's self-concept, and in turn adds a great deal of vitality to the sense of "self."

It should further be noted that the excesses of emotion expressed within a psychodramatic enactment are not likely to lead to a complete loss of control. The presence of the director and group, and the expectation of staying within limits act as influences to sustain a small amount of "observing ego" and "controlling ego" in the protagonist's personality. It is rare that a protagonist may begin to extend his destructiveness and stop "pulling his punches," and even then an experienced director can quickly regain control.

SURPLUS REALITY AND ROLE REVERSAL

Following the portrayal of many of the protagonist's fantasies, attitudes, and the fulfillment of act hunger, the protagonist has usually achieved a measure of insight into the nature of his own feelings. To this is now added an exploration of some of the other emotional dimensions of the situation.

For example, the adolescent who has explored some of his own conflicts about taking responsibility (and his externalizations of this conflict onto authority figures) may then portray his future. This is the use of *surplus reality* the dimensions of alternative past, present, and future events which are a "reality" in our imagination, if not in the outside world. In the *future projection technique,* the adolescent can enact his life five years in the future. The protagonist may discover that, as George Bernard Shaw once said, "There is only one thing worse than not getting what you want—and that is getting what you want!" Through future projection the protagonist can gain a more realistic approach, and begin to portray scenes in which he *can* achieve some successes based on his own work.

Another major form of utilizing surplus reality is to invite the protagonist to put himself in the place of the others in his life (role reversal). Through reversing roles (or changing parts) with the important figures in his psychodrama, the protagonist can develop some important practical and emotional insights into the others' situations. Thus, role reversal becomes a major technique for building the capacity for empathy with others. (Figure 19).

For example, in the psychodrama of Joe, the director may have the protagonist explore some of the others' feelings after his catharsis:

Director: Now, be your father . . .

Joe (as father): All right, I *admit* I did want you to be a football player, 'cause I never had the chance.

Director: Change parts.

Joe: (less whining): Well, Dad, that's your "trip." I have to do my own thing—I'm not going to make excuses for myself anymore.

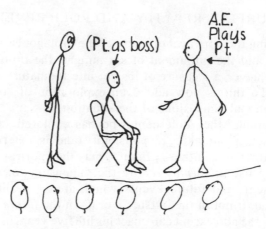

Figure 19

Later, the director may have Joe experience his employer's situation, and in the reversed role position, Joe considers the possibility that Mr. Jones is susceptible to pressures from his other subordinates, Joe's co-workers.

Joe (as Boss): Look, Joe, I really don't like being in this position . . .

Then Joe can be helped to creatively find some approaches that might support his boss and yet help his own position: a way of self-assertion in making tactful constructive suggestions.

In addition to the use of surplus reality and role reversal, the process of working through, or integration, involves behavioral practice, role training, sharing, discussion, and supportive closure. These dimensions and techniques will be discussed in the next chapter.

SUMMARY

The progress of a psychodrama can be visualized as following the pattern of a curve (Figure 20), as described by Barbara Seabourne and Carl Hollander:

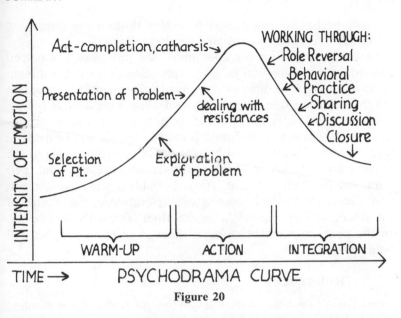

Figure 20

The implications of this construction are these:

As the protagonist approaches an apex of feeling, the resistances increase. He is always free to choose or refuse to explore further. This is established at the outset. As resistances grow, the director must continuously work mutually with the protagonist, and decide whether to allow for some distance, take an alternative route and work again another day, or attempt to work through the resistances and reach the point of emotional openness. (There are many sessions in which the protagonist is not ready to finish his exploration—"working sessions." There is no need for the director to feel that he must produce a dramatic catharsis in each enactment: this only leads to an undue "pushing" of the protagonist, instead of allowing him to grow at his own pace.)

Once the protagonist has reached a point of act completion, catharsis, or otherwise has seemed to achieve his peak of emotion, the director should allow him to move toward *less* emotional intensity (i.e., integration and closure). It becomes confusing if a protagonist attempts to follow one exploration with another.

Usually he has enough energy to deal with only one dimension of his life experience in any one session.

In summary, during the enactment, the protagonist is helped toward the gradual portrayal and exploration of the many dimensions of his life. The director attends to the protagonist's progress (1) from dealing with peripheral to dealing with central issues; (2) to portrayal of the spectrum of the protagonist's inner realities (for which reason psychodrama is called "the theater of truth"); (3) toward fulfillment of act hunger in act completion; (4) to the explicit presentation of internal attitudes and feelings, and their integration in "action insight"; (5) to possibly reaching a catharsis; and, finally (6) to the beginning of exploration of the worlds of the others in the protagonist's "social atom" through role reversal. In the next chapter, the *working through* of these insights will be discussed.

References

Allen, Doris Twitchell. Psychodrama in the crib. *Group Psychotherapy.* 1966, *19*(1-2), 23-28.

Allen, Doris Twitchell. Psychodrama in the family. *Group Psychotherapy,* 1954, *7*(1-2), 167-177.

Chapman, A. H. *Put-offs and come-ons.* New York: Berkeley Medallion Publishing, 1969.

Ellis, Albert. *Reason and emotion in psychotherapy.* New York: Lyle Stuart, 1962.

Hollander, Carl. *A process for psychodrama training: The Hollander psychodrama curve.* Littleton, Colo.: Evergreen Institute Press, 1969. Excellent pamphlet.

Laing, R. D. *Knots.* London: Tavistock Publication Ltd., 1970.

O'Connell, Walter. Adlerian psychodrama with schizophrenics. *Journal of Individual Psychology,* May 1963, *19,* 69-76.

Parrish, Marguerite, Psychodrama, description of application and reviews of technique. *Group Psychotherapy,* 1953, *6*(1-2), 74-77.

Perls, Frederick S. *Gestalt therapy verbatim.* Lafayette, Cal.: Real People Press, 1969.

Sacks, James M. The judgment technique. *Group Psychotherapy,* 1967, *20*(1), 29-31.

Sacks, James M. The judgment technique in psychodrama. *Group Psychotherapy,* 1965, 18(1-2), 69-72.

Schulman, Bernard. A psychodramatically oriented action technique in group psychotherapy. *Group Psychotherapy.* 1960. *13*(1-2), 34-38.

Seabourne, Barbara. Some hints on dealing with various kinds of pro-
    tagonists: Some rough notes. Unpublished manuscript, St. Louis State
    Hospital, 1966. Outstanding materials.
Shapiro, Stewart. Resistances to ego therapy. *Psychological Reports,*
    1960, *18,* 703.
Siroka, Robert and Schloss, Gilbert. The death scene in psychodrama
    Group Psychotherapy, 1968, *21*(4), 202-205.
Tobin, Stephen A. Saying goodbye in gestalt therapy. *Psychotherapy:
    Theory, Research and Practice,* 1971, *8*(2), 150-155.
Yablonsky, Lewis. The future-projection technique. *Group
    Psychotherapy* 1954, *7*(3-4), 303-305.

6

Working Through: Behavioral Practice, Sharing, and Closing

The third and last phase of psychodramatic enactment, following the warm-up and action portion, is the time for *working through*. The protagonist is ready to restore his general equilibrium by (1) developing some sense of mastery over his problem, (2) receiving group support while reconstituting his defenses, and (3) dealing with issues of reparation and "re-entry" into the outside world.

The challenge of mastery in working through may be one of the major tasks of the enactment. By mastery, I refer to the development of effective behavioral responses to a stressful situation. What approach would be the best in asking the boss for a raise? How can a protagonist deal with his mother when he returns home? What should a protagonist say to a friend who asks for an unreasonably demanding favor?

In psychodrama, the protagonist is helped to integrate the dimensions of his nonrational feelings into the decisions which concern these tasks. Ventilation, exploration, association, and catharsis may all be part of that process (as discussed in the previous chapter). However, in some settings (such as school or work) where personal disclosure is not appropriate, the task of finding better behavioral responses may nevertheless be approached through the media of *role-playing, sociodrama,* or *role training* (see Chapter 1). In these approaches, much of the personal exploration that was discussed in the previous chapter is not necessary. The working through portion occupies the major portion of the session's time, and consists primarily of *behavioral practice*.

In this chapter, I will discuss the techniques involved in behavioral practice, sharing, and closing.

BEHAVIORAL PRACTICE

The function of behavioral practice is to experiment with a variety of new behaviors (1) in a "fail-safe" context, (2) with feedback regarding the effectiveness of these trial behaviors, and (3) with opportunities for repeated attempts until some degree of satisfaction is achieved. These three components are invaluable in the protagonist's working through of his problem. The behavioral practice may or may not be associated with a deeper level of emotional exploration.

TECHNIQUES OF BEHAVIORAL PRACTICE

The first step in behavioral practice is setting up the enactment in the same way as described in the warm-up and the first part of the chapter on action. Once the situation is presented and the protagonist and auxiliary egos are involved in the scene, the director proceeds to get "feedback" on the protagonist's behavior.

The protagonist may simply be asked how he feels about his response, and how he might like to try it differently. Members of the group may also be asked for their observations and/or suggestions. Furthermore, group members may be invited to show how they would handle the situation in the enactment.

The protagonist role-reverses, and replays the scene, thus experiencing the situation from the other person's point of view. The auxiliary ego is instructed to act in the same way as the protagonist behaved, and thus the protagonist learns what it is like to be "on the receiving end" of his own behavior.

An auxiliary ego portrays the behavior of the protagonist, who steps out of the scene and observes. This is one form of the *mirror technique*. Group consensus is sought by the director to assure that the auxiliary ego's behavior is a fairly accurate portrayal of the protagonist's nonverbal style. If the group feels that the auxiliary ego is inaccurate, he is either given another chance to replay the scene and correct his behavior, or someone else can enact the scene as he saw it happen. Finally, the protagonist can re-enter the scene and try again. In many ways this is similar to the use of videotape in group psychotherapy.

After the protagonist receives feedback as to how he had been behaving, and some possible ideas as to how he might act differently, the director encourages him to repeatedly replay the scene until he finds a response that fits his own temperament, and meets the requirements of the situation to his own satisfaction.

For the protagonist who has difficulty creating a different response, the director can suggest that he try a behavior which would be "the worst possible response." Alternatively, the protagonist might be asked to behave in a way that would be totally different from his habitual style. Specifically, the protagonist may be directed to play the scene being silly, brutally frank, very cautious and indirect, or confrontational. Experimenting with these artificial manners gives the protagonist freedom to take a risk (because he was *told* to act that way), and to perhaps find that there are aspects of this new behavior which he might wish to integrate into his own style. For example, in a group setting, two of the participants in a nonverbal interaction exercise behaved in a very constricted fashion. After some discussion, the two people were asked to repeat the exercise in a way in which they would never behave in their everyday lives. They proceeded to interact in a silly, awkward, rough-and-tumble manner. Afterwards, they reported feeling foolish, but admitted that they enjoyed themselves tremendously. To their surprise, the group reinforced their risk-taking by feeding back that they were delighted with the two people's spontaneity.

Another approach to behavioral practice is for the director to suggest *specific* behaviors in the enactment, e. g., "Try asserting yourself while you stand with your pelvis tilted forward and your jaw thrust out"; "Answer your mother with the palms of your hands facing downwards instead of turned upwards in a pleading gesture."

It should be emphasized again that in psychodramatic enactments in which the protagonist's *self-understanding* is the major task, it is best to deal with issues of working through and behavioral practice only *after* the protagonist has first ventilated and explored the *meaning* of his emotions. Moreno notes: "Enactment comes first, retraining comes later. We must give [the protagonist] the satisfaction of act completion first, before considering retraining for behavior changes."

APPLICATIONS OF BEHAVIORAL PRACTICE

There are several subtypes of behavioral practice:

Professional skills training Skills in interviewing, history-taking, counseling, or giving support can all be developed with role-playing, e. g., What should one say to a dying patient? How does one ask about sexual issues in interviewing? What is the best response to an irritated or dissatisfied customer?

Assertion training This is a major area of behavior therapy in clinical psychology, e. g., How should one stand up to a dominating friend or resist peer pressures? How can one say "no" to a persistent salesman? How does one ask for a date? (this takes self-assertion); What is the best way to speak up at a meeting?

These methods can be used to help shy, constricted people become more forceful. In addition, behavioral practice can help histrionic, overly dramatic personalities to be less forceful or to develop more matter-of-fact and appropriate styles of relating.

Desensitization For those who tend to become easily flustered or frightened, repeated re-enactments of an anxiety-provoking situation in a supportive setting can reduce the avoidance response. In this context, behavioral practice is an action approach similar in spirit to Wolpe's "reciprocal inhibition" and other "deconditioning" approaches for phobias, impotence, and other psychological problems. Examples include preparation for confrontation in an encounter group; enacting the response to a fire in a home; building gradual, step-wise reactions to a sexually threatening situation.

Role training Related to the above-mentioned approaches, some groups can be helped with challenges of role transitions, e. g., chronically institutionalized psychiatric patients can be prepared for leaving the hospital by practicing situations of seeking employment, returning home, and even simple tasks such as opening a bank account or going on an airplane; parents-to-be can practice simulated bathing of the baby; a teenager who has recently had a colostomy can prepare for embarrassing questions from schoolmates; parents can explore different approaches to the management of behavior problems in their children.

Spontaneity training   The last major subtype of behavioral practice is the experimentation with *play* modalities. Many people have forgotten how to allow themselves to be spontaneous and playful. Opportunities to expand the imagined range of possible roles can extend the protagonist's sense of mastery over a variety of situations, e.g., playing roles of the hero, villain, tyrant, newborn baby, animal, tree, God, seductress, prima donna, etc. (See Chapter 9 on theory for more discussion of the place of spontaneity training.)

Thus behavioral practice in its many forms can serve as an invaluable aid in working through a problem. Trial behaviors are explored in a "fail-safe" context, and support and reinforcements are given to more appropriate responses.

SHARING

Once the protagonist has finished his enactment, he is in the process of becoming gradually more reflective, less warmed-up, and he is ready to receive some feedback. In the enactment, his physical involvement and spontaneity have rendered him very vulnerable to the judgments of the others in the group—much more vulnerable than if he had used only his verbal defenses in a narrative form. Instead of permitting a potentially humiliating "analysis," the director uses the psychodramatic technique of *sharing*. In sharing, the director seeks feedback which puts a premium on support and on the self-disclosure of the group members.

THE TECHNIQUE OF SHARING

The director leads the protagonist to the edge of the stage, and, (along with some of the auxiliary egos), sits down with him. The spontaneous feelings of closeness or the intuitive sense of the protagonist's needs determine how close people are to sit and whether body touching is appropriate (Figure 21).

Figure 21

Psychodramas which have produced a catharsis or a portrayal of a very moving situation sometimes close with hugging and shared crying among the group members and the protagonist. Other enactments in which the protagonist has made a "breakthrough" using the media of playfulness may close with triumphal activity or a rough-and-tumble joyous wrestling match. The primary guidelines for the director are based on the spontaneous, genuine feelings of the people involved, rather than the applications of any superficial technique.*

I discourage the ritualistic practice of applause after a psychodramatic enactment: I think it cheapens the whole process. (This is to be differentiated from an allowable spontaneous burst of joyous applause when something happens during an enactment which evokes the group's enthusiasm.)

---

*Dr. Robert Goulding notes that hugs and "strokes" should not be given when the protagonist is using the "need" or demand for these reinforcements as part of his manipulations, or in the service of what is termed by transactional analysis as his "racket." Rather, these expressions of warmth should be reserved for spontaneous responses to authentic behavior.

Once the protagonist is seated, the director explains *sharing* to the group:

"Now is the time for sharing. The protagonist (use his name, e.g., "Joe") has shared with you a very personal part of his life; he has left himself vulnerable to your comments. Rather than give an "analysis," it would be more appropriate for us to respond authentically and subjectively. How has Joe's drama touched each of you? What have *you* experienced that relates to Joe's situation?"

At this point, several people usually express past or present conflicts in their own lives, and share the mixed feelings that they too have felt. The auxiliary egos may also be invited to share the reactions they experienced "in role,"—i.e., as the protagonist's mother, brother, employer, as well as their own real life feelings.

Some group members tend to opinionate, however, e.g., "I felt you were being really hostile and that this is probably due to your relationship with your mother." (Because a sentence begins with "I feel" it is not prevented from being any less of an opinion.) The director should abruptly intervene and reiterate the instructions about sharing: "This is not the time to talk about *Joe's* problem. How has his story touched *your* life?" If others try to talk about their own feelings, but because of defensive habit, continue to say, "You feel . . ." or "You want . . ," the director may gently remind them of taking responsibility for their own statements: "You mean, 'I feel' don't you?" Usually the group member will respond quickly and proceed talking about his *own* experiences in the first person.

If no one in the group initiates the sharing, it could be due to several causes: (1) the group is not warmed up enough; (2) the group cohesion is still weak and others are afraid to disclose themselves; (3) the protagonist's enactment was too abstract or the situation too foreign to the group; (4) the protagonist's position was very different from group norms or values; or (5) the group is angry with the protagonist or director. Each situation must be dealt with creatively by the director.

One approach to resistance in the group's sharing is for the director to simply repeat that the protagonist has given each of them a "gift," and that it would be unfair for the group not to share in return.

In another approach, the director says, "Look around at the group . . . look at their eyes . . . they are telling you their feelings." Or, he can ask the protagonist, "Who do you think is touched by your story, and who is not?"

Sometimes the group may have a need to share not only with the protagonist, but also with the "person" played by one of the auxiliary egos—such as the protagonist's father or brother: "I feel for you, Mr. Smith, because I too have a son like Joe (the protagonist), and I felt the same way. . ." The director asks the group to share with the significant other person in the protagonist's life after the group shares with the protagonist. This technique can keep the end of the session in action and may allow for a more complete closure.

Most of the time, the sharing proceeds smoothly. Often the sharing by one of the other group members may lead directly into another psychodrama: "My mother never understood either; and I rejected her . . . and now she's dead!" (Weeps) The group member who shared now becomes the protagonist and is helped to enter his own enactment (he is already warmed up!). Indeed, a long session may have several psychodramas, each triggered by the other.

It is very important for both group members and the protagonist to have a time of sharing. Not only does this provide mutual support, but misunderstandings which may have arisen during the session can then be clarified through the opportunity for questions and feedback.

For example, in a role-playing session with nursery school teachers, the problem arose as to how to set up a conference with the resistant mother of an aggressive child. Several teachers in turn took the role of the one who was trying to coax, cajole, or firmly "instruct" the "mother" (played by one of the group members) to make an appointment. Finally, one of the teachers, Mary, risked being "too hard" and set down an ultimatum: "Either the mother comes in by a specified date or the child must leave the school." The teacher playing the mother became furious, and vigorously tongue-lashed Mary for this "unreasonable" position. The group broke into a burst of spontaneous applause. After the role-playing was over, there was no time left for sharing.

In the next session, a week later, Mary reported having experienced anxiety during the interval: she felt the group rejected her because of her stand. Mary felt that the rejection was "proved" by the group's applause at the angry response of the other teacher (as mother). The group was surprised, and vociferously reassured Mary that the applause was not *against* her; indeed, they felt her stance was most effective. The applause was for the *other* teacher's burst of spontaneous, "angry" emotion! It was not that the group agreed with the "mother," but that they were delighted with other teacher's open *expression of affect*—so hungry were they for some active, emotional interchange. Although Mary was pleased to receive this reassurance, she had still undergone a week of unnecessary worry. The director should have paced himself so that the sharing and feedback occurred right after the enactment.

In summary, the sharing period provides an opportunity for all the participants in a psychodrama to ventilate their feelings. The group members need this as much as the protagonist does. The catharsis in the drama may then spread, be re-experienced, and subside as the group realizes its common bond of human feelings.

CLOSING

At the end of a group session, the director may wish to finish with a variety of approaches. The length of the session, the degree of cohesion and self-disclosure achieved, and the task of the group are all variables to be considered. Often a period of discussion may follow the sharing, which could lead to a further "winding down" of the level of tension.

Some of the components of closing to be considered include the following:

1. *Dealing with "re-entry"* How will the group members adapt what they have learned to their everyday lives? This is

especially important after long "marathon" or otherwise intensive sessions, such as those experienced in encounter groups.

2. *Summarizing* In more task-oriented groups, where personal involvement has been limited, a summary of what has gone on and discussion of implications and plans may be in order.

3. *Planning the next session* In ongoing therapy groups, future agendas may be discussed. Perhaps one of the group specifically volunteers to be a protagonist, or it is agreed that a certain theme will be dealt with.

4. *Support* If one protagonist has become particularly vulnerable due to his participation and risk-taking in an enactment or confrontation, and the director feels he may need some additional support, he may wish to use a specific *ego building technique,* e.g., each person in the group tells the protagonist something he likes about him.

5. *Unfinished business* There may yet be a sense of unspoken feelings between group members (including the director). One technique is *resentments and appreciations:* "Before we close, we should ventilate any unfinished business. It's not always necessary to work these things out, but it's important that the unspoken feelings be expressed openly before we end." (The group is drawn into a circle:) "You may want to share directly the resentments and/or appreciations you feel for each other. Now is the time to do so." Then the group members speak up as they feel the need: "John, I resent the way you judged me"; "Bill, I appreciate your support, and resent your pity"; etc.

6. *Closing rituals* There are a variety of closing techniques which are adapted more for the end of encounter groups (e.g., chanting "om" while holding hands in a circle, a group guided fantasy, etc.). Some of these may be modified for a variety of group situations.

7. *Dealing with separation* The "intimacy" experienced in groups that have had much emotional exchange is often such a new experience to the group members that they resist letting go of the group cohesion. Ritualizing the separation experience can often be useful, e.g., the group forms a close circle and each

person is instructed to look at the other and say "goodbye" to every other person in the group. (It is not necessary to do this one at a time; all can do it simultaneously.)

SUMMARY

This chapter has discussed the activities of the third and last phase of the psychodramatic enactment. The working through of the problem using behavioral practice may either be a way of following up the insight or may itself dominate the session. Following the enactment, the director moves into the sharing phase, and finally closes, using a variety of techniques.

References

Feinberg, Henry. The ego building technique. *Group Psychotherapy,* 1959, *12*(3-4), 230-235.

Goldfield, M. Use of TV videotape to enhance the value of psychodrama. *American Journal of Psychiatry,* 1968, *125*(5), 690-692.

Heilbrun, Gert. On sharing. *American Journal of Psychotherapy,* 1967, *21*(4), 750.

Seabourne, Barbara. Role training. Unpublished manuscript, St. Louis State Hospital, 1966.

Speros, Tom. The final empty chair. *Group Psychotherapy,* 1972, *25*(1-2), 32-33.

Sturm, Israel Eli. The behavioristic aspects of psychodrama. *Group Psychotherapy,* 1965, *18*(1-2), 50-64.

Sturm, Israel Eli. Psychodrama in an adult education program. *Group Psychotherapy,* 1967, *20*(1-2), 181-183.

7

Principles and Pitfalls

The effective helping relationship is characterized by certain basic principles, which involve the development of the helper's sense of professional commitment and intellectual humility, as well as his forming a truly mutual relationship with his clients. These principles apply equally well to the leadership of any group in which human feelings are subject to expression and examination, irrespective of the method used. In the use of psychodrama, many pitfalls are possible whenever the principles which underlie the method are forgotten. In this chapter, I shall discuss some of these issues more fully.

THE CONTEXT OF MUTUALITY

The principle of mutuality refers to the wholehearted respect of the client as one who is growing and exploring in his own way. Within the group the sense of mutual trust can only grow when based on norms of respect. The director may comment on some of these norms in his introductory remarks:

During this group session, each of you will be responsible for choosing your own directions. You may proceed at your own pace. You will benefit from these sessions in direct proportion to your own active participation and the extent to which you are willing to take some risks.

My role is to help you clarify your goals and feelings. I can show you some methods which you may find helpful in re-defining your experiences more creatively. More importantly, in this group

I will attempt to develop an atmosphere in which you will feel ready to explore.

The purpose of this kind of introduction is to establish a norm of mutual trust and respect, which is in sharp contrast to the spirit of the "attack confrontation" which characterizes the worst kinds of contemporary small group practices. There is no place in group work for an attempt to tear down the client's defenses. This misguided approach only tends to increase the defensiveness of everyone in the group.

Another reason why the "attacking" approach is not appropriate in group settings is that the process of the group is in itself powerful enough to engender a great deal of motivation for exploration. The use of psychodramatic methods as warm-ups can greatly facilitate this process. The director can also use psychodramatic methods in later stages of the group process, in order to resolve conflicts and clarify issues. "Clever" interpretations and confrontations by the leader are relatively unimportant in the overall growth process. In other words, the *medium* of the use of group methods is the *message*.

Not only should the director himself avoid confrontational attacks, but he should also limit the tendency of group members to subtly attack each other. The practice of giving feedback when it is not asked for is often a form of externalization or projection on the part of the person making the interpretation. The director may identify the source of such thinly-veiled attacks by gently saying to the speaker, "You seem genuinely concerned about X's behavior. Would you care to explore what it is about *his* behavior that affects *you* so deeply?"

PROFESSIONAL HUMILITY

It is essential that the director have an awareness of the strengths and limitations of the many methods in helping personal development. Over the last decade, scores of innovations have been introduced into the fields of psychotherapy, education, and management. All too often the proponents of these new methods tend to idealize their pet approach. This leads to the pitfall of applying that method indiscriminately: those protagonists for whom a certain approach is ineffective may be coerced into useless efforts at staying with that method. The true professional knows that there are many varied populations which require different therapeutic or educational approaches.

Relating to this principle, some of the more specific cautions for the director to follow are to avoid idealizing certain terms and phrases, and condemning their opposites. Some currently "in vogue" cliches include: "feelings"; "experiencing"; "confrontation"; "do your own thing"; "you are responsible"; "the here-and-now"; "openness"; "honesty"; and so forth. Some of the terms which are presently taking on a negative connotation include: "defense"; "phoney"; "intellectual"; "discussion"; "analysis." Although the new values implicit in such semantic connotations do reflect some important emphases appropriate for the emerging human potential culture, these new terms are not sacred. There are times where the intellectual and cognitive must be applied to balance and synthesize the more emotional experiences.

PATHOLOGICAL SPONTANEITY

The principle of spontaneity can also be misused. Group leaders often deal with counter-transference reactions to a protagonist by getting angry at him, and then rationalize this behavior by calling it "being authentic," "modeling anger," "confrontation," or "feedback." Exhibiting any and all impulses is not the purpose of developing spontaneity. When grossly misused, this kind of expressiveness could be called *pathological spontaneity*.

The attacking behavior described above usually represents a form of acting-out of the director's own counter-transference (i.e., the therapist's emotional reaction to his patient). Another form of counter-transference behavior is the inappropriate use of undue physical contact, sexual advances, or sarcasm. The motivating forces for these types of behavior are manifold, and the director is cautioned to continuously assess his own behavior to prevent this most prevalent pitfall for all those in the helping role.

One of the most common sources of counter-transference behavior arises from the director's need to prove that he is professionally competent by obtaining "results." He thus becomes impatient with the realities of personal growth: its essentially *gradual* nature, fraught with resistances, defenses, and flagging motivation. If the director feels personally threatened, whether consciously or unconsciously, by his protagonist's slow progress or reactions, he is likely to engage in a variety of maneuvers: subtly provoking guilt, generally barraging his protagonist with words in an effort "to get a point across," nagging, and other confrontations. If the director is not aware of his counter-transference reactions, he may fall into the major error of pushing and coercing his clients, or allowing other group members to act out his own needs This is the source of most of the worst abuses prevalent in encounter groups and similar settings. These reactions also happen to the most experienced therapists, but at least they have learned to watch out for them.

ACTION VS. AWKWARDNESS

Although the director of a psychodramatic enactment should generally strive to keep the action going, he must nevertheless avoid the pitfall of trying too hard to attain technical virtuosity. It is much better to be awkward than to be clever. Indeed, as the late Dr. Wellman Warner wrote, "The response of an audience grows in inverse proportion to the smoothness of the production."* A truly polished enactment can be gained from the use of scripts and rehearsals, as is sometimes done in modified forms of creative dramatics—an error, in my opinion, because the use of rehearsed material loses the essential nature of psychodrama—its spontaneity. If spontaneity seems awkward, let it be: the group moves in to "help" the director.

Nevertheless, the director need not be self-consciously hesitant with statements such as, "Why don't you . . ."; "How would

* unpublished communication.

you feel about . . ."; "Would you like to . . ."; It is better to be gently positive. Once the freedom to say "no" has been clearly established, the director can speak with assurance: "Let's. . ."; "Be your father . . ."; "Show us . . ."

PROFESSIONAL CONSIDERATIONS

The director should be aware of the problems in leading different kinds of groups. The principles of working with hospitalized psychiatric patients are quite different from those involved in leading a personal development group. The following issues are but some of the challenges which should be carefully considered by any group leader:

1. *Selection*   The director should be aware of the problems inherent in including certain types of people in a group.

a. Those who are embroiled in life-crisis may dominate the group's attention unless they have someone else from whom they can receive counseling. It is not the purpose of a group session to take *full* responsibility for helping one of its members to make decisions about major life transitions, or to cope with losses. Of course, the group may serve as a useful *adjunct* in such cases.

b. Those who would likely become disruptive or unusually demanding should be carefully evaluated in the selection process, especially clients who are actively psychotic, depressed, histrionic, or intoxicated with a stimulant or psychedelic drug at the time of the group meeting.

c. Those who are attending the group *against* the advice of their therapist risk becoming psychiatric casualties. Another category of persons who are particularly vulnerable to the group process is the alienated and socially isolated who have no network of family or friends to which they return after the group.

d. Those who, against their better judgment, allow themselves to be overtly or covertly coerced into attending the group, e.g., those coming as part of an institutional in-service training program; as a requirement of work or at the request of a supervisor or employer; as part of an educational curriculum in order to obtain required credits; or under pressure from family, friends, or other helping persons in the community.

e. Those expecting a level of participation or self-disclosure which is different from the plans or expectations of the group leader or group. The director should see to it that the group knows his plans before they decide whether or not to attend (e.g., if he plans to go "deep," or to get into more intimate and personal issues, he should make this clear).

2. *Follow-up*   The director should be in such a position that he can assure that his group members will have access to further psychotherapy if needed. It is advisable for the director to have some psychiatric support—colleagues who can provide medication, hospitalization, or other forms of crisis intervention. Although these forms of follow-up are rarely needed, arranging for this "back-up" reflects the director's professional awareness of the nature of the impact of group process.

3. *Working with systems*   The director may be asked to lead a group of co-workers or students within an organization, e.g., a community agency, a business, a school system, and so forth. These situations require an awareness of some pitfalls involved with consultation to systems. It is also advisable for the director to be well-versed in principles of consultation before undertaking the leadership of such a group. Some of the pitfalls include the following:

a. When dealing with co-workers, the director should beware of the personal vulnerability which can be engendered through the use of action techniques. For this reason, it is often better to limit the use of psychodramatic methods to problem-oriented rather than personal-oriented approaches (i.e., using role-playing or sociodrama rather than psychodrama). It is rare that a group of those who live, work, or study together is so cohesive and free of internal competitiveness that it can tolerate the extensive, symmetrical self-disclosure that is required in the use of psychodrama. However, many psychodramatic methods can be adapted to these group situations.

b. The use of physical contact is an especially powerful modality and should be used with the greatest of caution. Among adolescents and other groups that are not well-versed in some of the norms of the encounter group methods, the use of touching and hugging tends to take on a distinctly sexual and/or threatening significance.

c. The group will often subtly manipulate the director into staging a scene dealing with co-worker (usually a supervisor) who is *not present*. "How do you deal with this person?" is the innocent topic of the role-playing. Actually, the director is being asked to ally against this person as the group works out its externalizations, displacements, and avoidance of self-examination. This is very similar to the pastime called "ain't it awful. . . ," described by Eric Berne in his book, *Games People Play*. The director should beware of this trap: the content of the session often backfires when it comes to the attention of the supervisor.

THE CLIENT-CENTERED SPIRIT OF PSYCHODRAMA

Much of what has been described in this chapter reflects an underlying philosophy which is essentially consistent with the spirit of Carl Rogers' "client-centered-therapy." It should be noted at the outset that the therapist need not be passive in order to engage mutually with his client. The term "nondirective," which has been used to describe Rogers' approach, refers to the therapist's avoidance of determining the *content* of the interaction. It is quite possible, however, for a therapist to be quite active and directive in helping his client to use a variety of *methods* to *explore* his problem. Thus, as in psychodrama, one can be directive in terms of *process* while still maintaining a true client-centered mutuality.

Rogers' most valuable contribution, in my opinion, has been his noting the essential conditions for an effective helping relationship, whatever the theoretical orientation of the helper. These conditions include (1) the authenticity of the way the therapist relates to his client; (2) the establishment of a bond of *empathy* between therapist and client; and (3) the therapist's development of a capacity for *positive regard* for his client. I find these principles to be profound, and I learn new facets and levels of these ideas as I continue to pursue the art of psychotherapy. Furthermore, Rogers' ideas are applicable to a variety of educational and psychotherapeutic methodologies, including the use of psychodramatic techniques. I would commend his writings to the reader for further study.

SUMMARY

When psychodramatic methods are used without the proper philosophical foundations, the director is in danger of falling into some common errors. These pitfalls can be avoided if the director applies certain basic principles which allow the person to develop at his own pace, in a context of mutuality, and without aggressive confrontation from the group leader. In short, they follow the conditions of client-centered therapy. The director must also remain aware of such group process issues as problems of selection and follow-up, the tendency to idealize one approach, and the ability of the director to tolerate ambiguity. It is hoped that the reader will continue to review his practice in light of these principles and pitfalls.

References
(see also References, Chapter 10)

Bach, Kurt W. *Beyond words*. New York: Russell Sage Foundation, 1971.

Beymer, Lawrence. Confrontation groups: Hula hoops? *Counselor Education and Supervision,* 1970, *9*(2), 75-86.

Blanchard, William. Ecstasy without agony is baloney. *Psychology Today,* 1970, *3*(8). Cautionary note on encounter groups.

Blank, Leonard. Confrontation techniques—A two-sided coin, in L. Blank and C. Gottsegen (Eds.) *Confrontation: Encounters in self and interpersonal awareness*. New York: Macmillan, 1971.

Freundlich, David. A psychoanalytic hypothesis of change mechanisms in encounter groups. *International Journal of Group Psychotherapy,* 1971, *23*(1), 42-53.

Hurewitz, Paul. Ethical considerations in leading therapeutic and quasi-therapeutic groups: Encounter and sensitivity groups. *Group Psychotherapy,* 1970, *23*(1-2), 17-20.

Kuehn, John L. and Crinella, Francis. Sensitivity training: Interpersonal "overkill" and other problems. *American Journal of Psychiatry,* 1969, *126*(12), 840-845.

Rogers, Carl R. *On becoming a person*. Boston: Houghton-Mifflin, 1961.

Rogers, Carl R. *Carl Rogers on encounter groups*. New York: Harper & Row, 1971.

Ross, W. D., Kligfeld, M., and Whithers, R. Psychiatrists, patients and sensitivity groups. *Archives of General Psychiatry*, 1971, 25(2), 178.

Siroka, Robert W., Siroka, E., and Schloss, G. (Eds.) *Sensitivity training and group encounter*. New York: Grosset and Dunlap, 1971.

Winthrop, Henry. Abuses of sensitivity training on American campuses. *Bulletin of Menninger Clinic*, 1971, 35(1), 128-141.

Yalom, Irvin. *Theory and practice of group psychotherapy*. New York: Basic Books, 1970

8

Applications of Psychodramatic Methods

Psychodramatic techniques may be effectively used in any field which requires some exploration of the psychological dimensions of a problem. The fields of education, psychotherapy and industrial relations have discovered that approaches which integrate participatory, experiential learning with verbal and cognitive analysis are the most beneficial for a program which aims at fully involving their clients in mutual explorations of multidimensional problems. This chapter will note some of the major categories of the contexts in which psychodramatic methods are currently being applied. Of course, each director must modify the methodology in order to meet the needs of his own style and ability, as well as the situation of the client and the realities of his helping role.

I. THE MENTAL HEALTH PROFESSIONS

The most common area in which psychodramatic methods are applied is in the field of mental health. In hospitals, clinics, day-care centers, crisis units, alcohol and drug programs, therapeutic communities, and many other settings, all kinds of professionals may find a role for psychodramatic methods in their therapeutic armamentarium. Sometimes psychodrama itself is used as a distinct program, or as part of the adjunctive treatment, along with occupational or recreational therapy. More often, methods and techniques derived from psychodrama are integrated into the process of individual, group, and conjoint family therapy (Fig. 22).

98

In group therapy, enactments of varying lengths may be interspersed with periods of discussion. Action methods (such as those mentioned in the chapter on warm-ups) can often be woven into the ongoing group process. Especially effective are the techniques of doubling, role reversal, or the interjection of an exercise of nonverbal communication. These function to circumvent some of the verbal impasses which occur so often in therapy groups.

For example, at one point in a group session, the members became involved in a series of abstract generalizations about philosophical issues. They seemed to have lost their sense of direction. The conversation was sparse and full of platitudes, and the members were no longer in touch with their own concerns and needs. The director threw a book of matches onto the floor in the middle of the group and told them that this was to be a symbol of something they all wanted, even though they might not be clear on just what that was. They were asked to physically deal with the matchbook, as if it were that valuable "something" they desired. One member picked it up, played with it, then gave it to another. A variety of responses followed: a sequence of giving, grabbing, tearing, holding, offering and rejecting the book of matches. After a few minutes, the action was stopped; the result was that the group felt it had quite a bit to talk about: why one person used the matches one way, and how another person reacted in a different fashion. The group began to talk about their interactional styles, their associations to the symbol, and their feelings about the way they had dealt with it. (In a different group, when a small object did not receive a quick warm-up, a chair was introduced as the symbol; since it necessitated more work to manipulate a chair, the corresponding increase in physical involvement led to a great deal of group interaction.)

Another group problem is the situation in which a member or a subgroup is dissatisfied or planning to leave the group. The spectogram is a psychodramatic technique which can be used to clarify the issues and illustrate the feelings of the group, placing those feeling one way on one side of the room, those feeling a different way on the other side, and those who are indifferent in the middle (Kole). This is followed by a discussion about any or all of the subgroups and it helps to minimize the anxiety of members who feel that they are the only ones in the group who feel the way they do. In groups dealing with a member of a subgroup who wants to leave, the facilitator may use the *behind-your-back* technique. Using this technique, those who wish to leave may symbolically do so by turning their back, and the rest of the group is instructed to discuss their leaving as if it had actually happened. (It should be noted that the *behind-your-back technique* can be very powerful and potentially destructive method of confrontation unless used with skill and judgment.) As the group talks, those who have "left the group" may be tempted to re-enter the group in order to correct misunderstandings and represent their case. They might also hear that there are others in the group who sympathize with them and defend them, and this too may induce them to return. In either case, the technique offers a shared experience that the group will then be able to discuss with an increased feeling of cohesion.

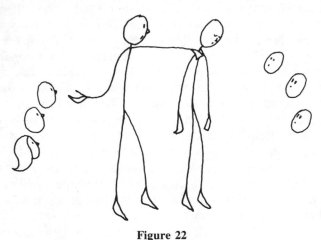

Figure 22

A third example occurred in a therapy group with adolescents. Joe, a young man, was explaining his tendency to joke and be superficial in his relationships with others. He said that he was aware that he was not letting himself become "close." Joe explained that if he were to be rejected after he had allowed himself to really care about another person, he was afraid he would be deeply hurt. He said that he wouldn't be able to stand it. The therapist had Joe recreate the situation and then helped him enact the feelings of one who is rejected, e.g., the questions as to his own guilt, the fears of being rejected for something about himself that he couldn't change, and so forth. In facing these issues, Joe learned that being rejected need not result in a catastrophic injury to one's self-esteem; indeed, although he was hurt, he was strong enough not to break down. This sense of inner strength was an enjoyable alternative to Joe's rationalized avoidance of closeness, and was reinforced by the group norm of not having to treat each other with "kid gloves."

In similar ways, this technique can be used to enact threats of loss of control over love, anger, grief and other emotions, as well as other excuses for avoiding goal-directed behavior. The result of these enactments, in which the fear is faced, results in an increasing sense of self-control.

In family therapy and marital counseling, psychodramatic methods can escalate the interchange to a more confrontational level of emotional encounter, which in turn facilitates a more meaningful exploration of the problems in the relationships among the participants.

For example, in some marital couple therapy meetings it becomes apparent that an "adversary system" has been established in the couple's relationship; that is, each partner seems to be trying to "win" by justifying himself and blaming the other. In this situation, each partner emphasizes what the other partner does that he *does not* like. In such confrontations, I have utilized the technique of role reversal, directing each person to take the part of his spouse. Then, I address each person with his spouse's name and ask him in-role to tell the partner, not what he doesn't want, but rather what he *does* want. If it seems that the person caricaturizes his partner by demanding the obviously impossible, I point this out, and encourage a more realistic portrayal. This approach, I found, has frequently "broken" the mental set in which each partner views the other as "uncaring," "selfish," or "withholding."

An anecdote is told about an episode which helped Dr. Moreno realize some of the therapeutic potentials of improvisatory drama:*

Barbara, one of Moreno's actress friends, was married to a young playwright, George. Barbara always portrayed gentle, wistful ingenues. But, according to what George confided in desperation to Moreno, at home she was a hellcat who cursed and kicked him when he tried to make love to her. The day of the next performance the newspapers reported the murder of a streetwalker by her pimp. Convincing Barbara she should broaden her range, Moreno cast her as the streetwalker. She played the part with such ferocity, rousing the actor who played the pimp to such a frenzied response, that at the climatic murder scene the audience stood up, screaming, "Stop!" At home after the show, temporarily purged of her aggressions, Barbara was all tenderness. Moreno kept her playing violent characters, and she grew tractable away from the theater. He then put George on the stage opposite her to duplicate episodes of their private life. 'Some months later,' he recounts, 'they sat with me in the theater, full of gratitude. They had found themselves and each other.'

II. PSYCHODRAMATIC METHODS
WITH CHILDREN AND ADOLESCENTS

Psychodramatic techniques are utilized to help young people explore the emotional conflicts in their lives at all age levels, and in all contexts—in the home, the child-guidance clinic, residential treatment centers, speech and hearing clinics, nursery schools, recreation centers, summer camps, the classroom and *in-situ* (i.e., on the spot, wherever the situation arises), on the playground, or the front yard, etc., (Figure 23).

In addition, psychodramatic methods, when modified for the

---

* This episode occurred when Moreno was staging scenes in his "theater of spontaneity," in Vienna, around 1921: situations from the popular press were often enacted as a kind of "living newspaper." Ref: Kobler, John, "The Theater that heals men's minds." The *Saturday Evening Post,* 27 October, 1962.

IN SITU:

Figure 23

setting, can be remarkably effective for children with relatively poor cognitive and verbal skills—such as the mentally retarded or pre-adolescent delinquents. Indeed, the use of role-playing techniques is a valuable approach to *building* verbal skills in these action-prone children.

Furthermore, psychodramatic techniques can be integrated with other forms of activity, play, and story telling therapies.

III. APPLICATIONS IN PRIMARY AND SECONDARY EDUCATION

Psychodramatic methods can be applied in many different school settings. Most of the time, the use of these methods should be limited to role-playing or sociodrama. This is because the more personal explorations which are involved in psychodrama may lead to too much self-disclosure for the protagonist in a context of peers.

In some of the following contexts the teacher or counselor can make good use of psychodramatic methods:

1. *Discussion of class material,* i.e., historical, literary, or contemporary social problems. Classes on the more complex personal relations involved in modern sex education programs may use role-playing materials to explore dating and marriage relationships, "constructive fighting," etc.

2. *Creative dramatics* is a field which is receiving widespread attention in many contemporary school settings, especially in Great Britain. However, the effectiveness of creative dramatics is in direct proportion to the degree to which the children are allowed to throw away their scripts and begin to improvise.

3. *Special situations*   Community crises relating to interracial strife, drug abuse programs, parent-student conflicts, or other issues of current attention can often become the focus of a socio-drama in a classroom or at an entire school assembly.

4. *Special education*   In special classes for children with learning disabilities, psychodramatic methods are used to help with the common problems of defeatism, behavior problems, and poor self-esteem. These special education classes include children who have specific learning disabilities, are severely emotionally disturbed or psychotic, or have behavior problems of hyperactivity.

A common theme of concern to children in special education is that of being "different." This problem can be dealt with using role-playing as part of group discussions. Other children who can benefit from exploring the emotional aspects of their disease are those with asthma, diabetes, deafness, blindness, or other crippling handicap.

5. *Affective education*   One of the most important developments in contemporary education is the attention being given to affective education, i.e., the development of coping skills in interpersonal relationships and understanding feelings in oneself. Certainly, the use of psychodramatic methods can catalyze this education for human awareness.

Unfortunately, the borderline between class discussion and destructive encounter group methods for personal development is still somewhat blurred. Anyone considering the idea of sensitivity-training or encounter in their classroom work should be aware of the many abuses in such new methods. It is quite sufficient to stay on relatively impersonal issues when teaching psychology and related materials in a school setting (see Chapter 7).

The use of psychodramatic methods in the schools has many potential benefits, if the approach is modified appropriately to the task at hand.

IV. PROFESSIONAL TRAINING

An important area for the applications of psychodramatic methods is in the development of interpersonal skills and sensitivity for students in training for the helping professions. Teachers, nurses, pastors, policemen, medical students, and many other groups can best deal with some items in their training through experiential rather than didactic modes of education (Figure 24).

Figure 24

For example, the problems of death and bereavement in our culture was one of the items brought up in a postgraduate development program for a group of nursery school teachers at the Child Psychiatry Clinic of The Cedars-Sinai Medical Center, in Los Angeles. Using psychodrama, the experience of grieving was explored. One teacher in the group started by asking how to deal with a child's questions about death. This led to another one of the teacher's enacting the loss of a spouse, which catalyzed a dramatic and emotion-filled catharsis by many of the teachers as they shared their own experiences of mourning. The results were: (1) a heightening of each group member's ability to help others with bereavement by using the empathy which arises from the person's contact with his own deep feelings; (2) an awareness of the importance of sharing the experience, talking about the feelings of grief rather than avoiding the issue, and of the need for touching and physical contact; and (3) an increased tolerance and opennesss not only to the experience of grief in the group members themselves and others, but also tolerance for the defenses against the expression of grief. These experiences enabled the group members to relate to the children and each other with greater authenticity.

Certainly, the problem of learning to help others grieve demands an experiential form of training. Nurses, medical personnel, and anyone else who must deal with this reality in their work could benefit from understanding the stressful situation through role-playing.

Not only is the problem of bereavement an issue for experiential training, but the problem of learning to help others with any complex role transition is a challenge in education. The plight of the young mother, the father of his first newborn, the man who has suffered a small stroke, the prospect of compulsory retirement are all subjects which involve a wide range of status changes and the demand for shifts in role behavior and values. Those who are in training for positions in which they will be helping people with life crises such as these would, I believe, benefit from participating in role-playing situations which are part of discussion seminars.

V. APPLICATIONS IN INDUSTRY

Psychodrama itself would rarely be appropriate for most work situations, for the same reason that one should not use psychodrama or deep encounter group methods in the classroom; a context with co-workers usually has more internal competition and distrust than people may wish to admit to themselves. Limited applications of psychodramatic methods, however, such as the use of role-playing and action techniques are widely used in industrial psychological consulting. The National Training Laboratories, which work with management and systems issues as well as sensitivity training issues, use many excellent techniques derived from psychodrama.

As in the fields of professional training, the major application of role-playing in industry is to develop the skills of managers, personnel workers, and salesmen. In addition, sociodramatic skills are often useful in resolving some of the more informal management-labor conflicts or other difficulties in communication. Most important, however, is the challenge of developing a sense of humanistic orientation, a broader imagination as to the implications of industry's actions in contemporary society and the building of psychological-interpersonal sophistication in management.

A director must be very aware of the subleties of working as a consultant to an organization. Those who would introduce sensitivity training into industry should become aware of the difficulties of organizational consultation. Many untrained, self-styled consultants who use group methods have left in their wake a series of damaged businesses and careers. The potential director of role-playing in an organization must become aware of the fundamental principles of consultation, the different needs of his clients, and the many competing agendas of the group with which he works (see Chapter 7). Nevertheless, if the management consultant is well-trained, his skills can be vastly extended by his knowledge of the appropriate psychodramatic methods which can be applied to his work.

VI. APPLICATIONS IN THE HUMAN POTENTIAL MOVEMENT (ENCOUNTER GROUPS)

The human potential movement in America is mainly characterized by the use of small group methods in order to facilitate personal development. The term "encounter group" will be used to refer to that genre of group activities including sensitivity training, T-groups, marathon groups, "Joy" workshops, the programs at growth centers, and others.

In these activities, psychodramatic methods are frequently used, and abused. Nevertheless, the role of psychodramatic methods in encounter groups will probably increase, and should be noted.

Psychodramatic methods can have a powerful impact on the process of an encounter group. Most of the techniques which are being utilized in comtemporary groups have their origins in Moreno's work.*

Psychodramatic methods serve the process of the encounter group in two ways. First, they function to clarify interpersonal difficulties; their use is essentially similar to the applications in group psychotherapy, as noted earlier in this chapter.

A more significant application of psychodramatic methods is in their function of warming-up group members to looking at their own "blind spots," and motivating them to deal with these problems. The use of action warm-ups has the important advantage of rapidly moving group members towards an awareness of their own problems, often without the necessity of having to be verbally confronted by other group members. Thus, the tone of attack groups can be converted to a more gentle philosophy

---

* Eric Berne wrote: "In his selection of specific techniques, Dr. Perls shares with other 'active' psychotherapists the 'Moreno problem': The fact that nearly all known 'active' techniques were first tried out by Dr. J. L. Moreno in psychodrama, so that it is difficult to come up with an original idea in this regard." From a review of Gestalt Therapy Verbatim, *American Journal of Psychiatry,* 126(10: 15-20,), April 1970.

A.H. Maslow (the "dean" of American humanistic psychology) wrote (regarding) Jane Howard's article on Esalen and other new developments in education and psychotherapy, "I would however like to add one credit-where-credit-is-due footnote. Many of the techniques set forth in the article were originally invented by Dr. Jacob Moreno, who is still functioning vigorously and probably still inventing new techniques and ideas." (Letter to Editors, LIFE Magazine, August 2, 1968).

Dr. William Schutz (a major figure in the American encounter group movement), noted that ". . . Virtually all of the methods that I had proudly compiled or invented [Moreno] had more or less anticipated, in some cases forty years earlier. . .", "Leuner's original article (on guided fantasy) has appeared in (Moreno's) Journal in about 1932, and he had been using the method periodically since . . . I invite you to investigate Moreno's work. It is probably not sufficiently acknowledged in this country. Perl's Gestalt Therapy owes a great deal to it. It is imaginative and worth exploring." (*Here Comes Everybody,* Harper & Row, 1971.)

which allows each participant to explore whatever he wishes *at his own pace* (Figure 25).

Figure 25

Not only psychodrama, but also many other methods are interwoven in the contemporary encounter group, in order to deal with a wide variety of dimensions of personal development (see Table 1 on page 111). Some of the major methods of developing personal growth are: (1) psychodrama and its derivatives; (2) bioenergetics, massage, and related "body" approaches; (3) Gestalt therapy and existential-humanistic ideas; (4) guided fantasy and psychosynthesis; (5) sensory awakening techniques; and (6) the use of creative media: improvisatory dance, art, theater games, music, etc.

Many of the references on the applications of psychodramatic methods and current developments in encounter groups may be found at the end of Chapters 7 and 10.

VII. APPLICATIONS IN RELIGION

One of the most exciting areas of application of psychodramatic and other group methods is in the field of religion. Many of the innovative approaches in religion today are adapted from the human potential movement, which has become *spiritual* in its focus, as well as interpersonal. The impact of many religious ideas from Oriental philosophies, the writings of the mystics, and even of some radical modern theologians, is now being felt in many local parishes. Certainly, the psychedelic movement of the late 1960s has galvanized a new interest among many young people—an interest both within and outside the confines of established religion. In response, many ministers are attempting to integrate the new ideas on religion in their counseling, sermons, and youth programs. (Encounter groups are often held under the aegis of a church.) Not only new ideas, but also new methods, such as psychodrama, are being utilized in order to bring issues of ultimate concern more vividly into the awareness of the parishioners in many churches.

It is interesting to note that Moreno's ideas about creativity and spontaneity were first reflected in his poetic and *theological* works, which were written before he ever developed the psychodramatic method as a psychotherapeutic technique. Moreno's writings about the dynamic encounter between man and God in a co-creative relationship take on new relevance today, as contemporary religious trends expand to include ideas from other philosophies, and the works of Carl Jung.

Moreno's word for enactments which deal with ultimate values and concerns is *axiodrama*. Through modifications of psychodramatic methods, a minister can search for more vivid and personal ways to help his parishioners or students to experience the challenge and significance of prayer, meditation, death, ethics, and so forth.

Some possible enactments or situation tests that could be used as an introduction to a religious psychodrama include: (1) the relationship between Jesus and Judas; (2) the Grand Inquisitor (Dostoyevsky's story within *The Brothers Karamazov*); (3) the judgment in Heaven (Chapter 5); (4) creation of a ritual for Christmas that is personally meaningful; or (5) the encounter between David and Absalom, Adam and Eve, and so forth.

In summary, psychodramatic methods can be applied in order to achieve many kinds of goals and in a variety of contexts.

This chapter has presented some of the major categories in which psychodramatic methods can be used, as well as providing references related to each area of application.

Table 1

Dimensions of Personal Development Which May be Enhanced through the Use of Psychodramatic Methods

SELF-AWARENESS

Clarification of inner feelings, goals, strengths, weaknesses, needs, fears

Growth of a wider role-repertoire, more realistic body-image, awareness of one's own interpersonal style, habitual responses

Sense of responsibility and ego boundaries strengthened

INTERPERSONAL SKILLS

Greater capacity for trust, autonomy, initiative, self-disclosure, self-assertion

Increased awareness of other people's weaknesses, fears, needs, temperamental differences

Knowledge of some common interactional and semantic communication difficulties; ability to express self congruently and clearly

The ability to listen, empathize, with less distortion

VALUE-SYSTEMS

Philosophy of life, some idea about the meaning of one's own death, significance of his life, relations with "spiritual" concerns, engagement in nonrational experiences, meditation

SPONTANEITY

Playfulness, improvisation, participation in art, song, dance, drama, humor, wonder

SENSORY-AWAKENING

Body movement, sense of rhythm, points of balance, appropriate use of touch and sensuality

IMAGINATION

Cultivation of skills in using associations, dreams, symbols, images, guided fantasy, intuition, story-telling, in personal growth

References

Applications in Mental Health Fields

A. Inpatient psychiatric services

Baker, A. A. The misfit family—a psychodrama technique used in a therapeutic community.*British Journal of Medical Psychologists*, 1952, *25*, 235-243.

Bell, R. Systematic role-playing teaches social skills. *Hospital and Community Psychiatry*, 1970, *21*(2), 189-191.

Chase, Philip and Farnham, Beverly. Psychodrama in a mental hospital. *Mental Hygiene*, 1966, *50*, 262.

Daly, Dennis C. Psychodrama as a core technique in milieu therapy. Unpublished doctoral dissertation, St. Louis University, 1961.

Deane, William N. and Hanks, Vera. Psychodrama in a mental hospital. *Group Psychotherapy*, 1967, *17*(1-2).

Gonen, Jay. The use of psychodrama combined with videotape playback on an inpatient floor. *Psychiatry*, 1971, *34*(2), 198-213.

Jones, Maxwell. *The therapeutic community*. New York: Basic Books, 1953. Comments on the use of psychodrama in the therapeutic milieu.

Ossorio, A. and Fine, Leon. Psychodrama as a catalyst for social change in a mental hospital, in J. Masserman and J. L. Moreno (Eds.) *Reviews and integrations*, Volume 5 of *Progress in psychotherapy*. New York: Grune and Stratton, 1960.

Polansky, Norman A. and Harkins, E. B. Psychodrama as an element in hospital treatment. *Psychiatry*, 1969, *32*(1), 74-87.

Rabiner, Charles J. and Drucker, M. Use of psychodrama with hospitalized schizophrenic patients. *Diseases of the Nervous System*, January 1967, *28*, 34.

Sackles, Constantine. The place of psychodrama in an inpatient psychiatric treatment program. *Group Psychotherapy*, 1968, *21*(4), 235-240.

Solomon, M. L. et al. Psychodrama as an ancillary therapy on a psychiatric ward. *Canadian Psychiatric Association Journal*, August 1970, *15*, 365-373.

Williams R. L. and Gasdick, J. M. Practical applications of psychodrama and chronic patients. *Hospital and Community Psychiatry*, 1970, *21*(2), 192-193.

B. Alcoholism

Blume, Sheila, Robins, Joan, and Branston, Arthur. Psychodrama techniques in therapy of alcoholism. *Group Psychotherapy*, 1968, *21*(4), 241-246.

Catanzaro, R. J. Tape-a-drama in treating alcoholics. *Quarterly Journal Studies in Alcoholism*, 1967, *28*(1), 138-140.

Olson, Peter and Frankhauser, Jerry. The B.U.D. and its resolution through psychodrama. *Group Psychotherapy and Psychodrama*, 1970, *23*(3-4), 84-90.

Weiner, Hannah. Psychodramatic treatment for the alcoholic, in Ruth Fox (Ed.) *Alcoholism: Behavioral research, therapeutic approaches*. New York: Springer Publishing, 1967.

Weiner, Hannah. Treating the alcoholic with psychodrama. *Group Psychotherapy*, 1965, *18*(1-2), 27-29. Good bibliography.

C. Outpatient group psychotherapy

Bach, George. *Intensive group psychotherapy*. New York: Ronald Press, 1954. Excellent review of the basics, primarily verbal methods, although he does mention some action techniques.

Corsini, Raymond J. Behind your back technique. *Group Psychotherapy*, 1954, *6*(1-2), 102-109.

Gerber, Lane. Integrating encounter technique into individual psychotherapy. *American Journal of Psychotherapy*, 1972, *26*(2), 257-262.

Lawlor, Russell. Psychodrama in group psychotherapy. *Sociometry*, 1946, 9(3-4), 275.

Seeman, Kenneth. Multimodality outpatient group psychotherapy. *American Journal of Psychotherapy*, 1968, *22*(3), 443-459.

Steele, Robert E. and Nash, Kermit. Sensitivity training and the black community. *American Journal of Orthopsychiatry*, 1972, *42*(3), 424-430.

Strean, H. S. Nonverbal interaction in psychotherapy. *Psychotherapy: Theory, Research and Practice*, 1969, *6*(4), 235-238.

Also, many of the "encounter" techniques which are part of marathon groups and warm-ups can be found in REFERENCES, Chapters 4 and 10, and elsewhere in the book.

D. Family therapy

Allen, Doris Twitchell. Psychodrama in the family. *Group Psychotherapy*, 1954, *7*(1-2), 167-177.

Jacobson, Clarissa and Mann, Joseph. Family in treatment. *Group Psychotherapy*, 1962, *15*(1), 46-51.
Knoblochova, J. and Knoblochova, F. Family therapy in Czechoslovakia: An aspect of group-centered psychotherapy, in Nathan Ackerman (Ed.) *Family therapy in transition*. Boston: Little, Brown, 1970. Also other articles in this volume which comment on integration of psychodramatic and role-playing methods in family therapy, multiple family group therapy, etc.
Liss, Jerome. *Family talk*. New York: Ballantine Books, Inc., 1972.
Starr, Adeline. Psychodrama with a family. *Group Psychotherapy*, 1959, *12*(1).

E. Child psychotherapy and "in the home"

Anzieu, Didier. Aspects of analytic psychodrama applied to children. *International Journal of Sociometry and Sociatry*, 1958, *1-2*, 42-47.
Bodwin, R. Use of psychodrama in a psychiatric clinic. *Group Psychotherapy*, 1954, *6*(4), 222-226.
Borden, R. Use of psychodrama in an institute for delinquent girls. *Sociometry*, 1940, *3*(91-2), 81.
Boulanger, J. B. Group analytic psychodrama in child psychiatry. *Canadian Psychiatric Association Journal*, 1965, *10*(5), 427-432.
Drabkovna, H. Experiences resulting from clinical use of psychodrama with children. *Group Psychotherapy*, 1966, *16*(1-2), 32-36.
Gardner, Richard A. The mutual storytelling technique. *American Journal of Psychotherapy*, 1970, *24*(3), 419-439.
Goodman, Jerome M. Nondirective psychodramatic play therapy. *American Journal of Orthopsychiatry*, 1962, *32*, 532-534.
Kors, Pieter C. Unstructured puppet shows as group procedures in therapy with children. *Psychiatric Quarterly Supplement*, 1964, *38*(1), 56-75.
Lippitt, Rosemary. Psychodrama in the home. *Sociatry*, 1947, *1*(2), 166.
Lippitt, Rosemary. Psychodrama in the kindergarten and nursery school. *Group Psychotherapy*, 1954, *7*(4), 262-290.
London, P. and Madsen, C. H., Jr. Role-playing and hypnotic susceptibility in children. *Journal of Personal and Social Psychology*, September 1968, *10*, 66-68.
Smilansky, Sarah. *The effects of sociodramatic play on disadvantaged pre-school children*. New York: John Wiley and Sons, 1968.
Starr, Adeline. The role of psychodrama in a child guidance clinic. *Individual Psychology Bulletin*, 1951, *9*, 18-24.
Strean, H. S. Treating parents of emotionally disturbed children through role-playing. *Psychoanalysis and Psychoanalytic Review*, 1960, *47*(1), 67-76.
Verven, N., Waldfogel, S., and Young, R. A. Modified psychodrama

and group psychotherapy in a treatment camp. *International Journal of Group Psychotherapy*, 1956, *6*, 291-299.

F. Adolescents and delinquency

Deeths, Adele. Psychodramatic crisis intervention with delinquent drug users. *Group Psychotherapy*, 1970, *23*(1-2), 41-45.

Eliasoph, Eugene. Role training and psychodrama in group psychotherapy with adolescent drug addicts. *Group Psychotherapy*, 1955, *8*(3-4), 308-315.

Godenne, Ghislaine D. Outpatient adolescent group psychotherapy and psychodrama. *American Journal of Psychotherapy*, 1965, *19*(1), 40.

Goldman, Elaine and Goldman, S. Group psychotherapy and psychodrama with urban disadvantaged youth, *Group Psychotherapy*, 1968, *21*(4), 206-210.

Haskell, Martin. The drug addict, role-playing and group psychotherapy—the need for a new approach. *Group Psychotherapy*, 1958, *11*(3-4), 197-202.

Head, Wilson A. Sociodrama and group discussion with institutionalized delinquent adolescents. *Mental Hygiene*, 1962, *46*(1), 127-135.

Herman, Leon. An exploration of psychodrama with institutionalized delinquents. *Group Psychotherapy*, 1968, *21*(4), 211-213.

Lebovici, Serge, Diatkine, R. and Kestenberg, E. Psychodrama as applied to adolescents. *Journal of Child Psychology and Psychiatry*, 1961, *1*, 298 305.

Miller, M. M. Psychodrama therapy in juvenile court. *Journal of Criminology and Criminal Law*, 1960, *50*, 453.

Yablonsky, Louis. Sociopathology of the violent gang and its treatment, in J. Masserman and J. L. Moreno (Eds.) *Reviews and integrations*, Volume 5 of *Progress in psychotherapy*. New York: Grune and Stratton, 1960.

Zacharias, J. Psychodrama with teenagers. *Group Psychotherapy*, 1966, *18*(4).

G. Mental retardation

Fliegler, L. A. Play acting with the mentally retarded. *Exceptional Children*, 1952, *19*, 56-60.

Newburger, H. Psychodrama treatment with the brain damaged. *Group Psychotherapy*, 1967, *20*(3), 129-130.

Pankratz, Loren and Buchan, G. Techniques of warm-ups in psychodrama with the retarded. *Mental Retardation*, 1966, *4*(5), 12-16.

Pilkey, L. et al. Psychodrama and empathic ability in the mentally retarded. *American Journal of Mental Deficiency*, 1961, *65*, 595-605.

Sarbin, Theodore R. Spontaneity training of the feeble-minded, in C.

L. Stacey and De. Martino (Eds.) *Counselling and psychotherapy with the mentally retarded.* New York: Free Press, 1957.

Taylor, J. F. Role-playing with borderline and mildly retarded children in an institutional setting. *Exceptional Children,* 1969, *36,* 206-208.

H. Speech problems

Clayton, Lynette and Robinson, L. D. Psychodrama with deaf people. *American Annals of the Deaf,* 1971, *116*(4), 415-419.

Schlanger, P. H. and Schlanger, B. B. Adapting role-playing activities with aphasic patients. *Journal of Speech and Hearing Disorders,* 1970, *35*(3), 229-235.

Webster, H. Procedures for group parent counseling. *Journal of Speech and Hearing Disorders,* 1968, *33*(2), 128-131.

Wolpe, Zelda. Play therapy, psychodrama, and parent counseling, in L. E. Travis (Ed.) *Handbook of speech pathology.* New York: Appleton-Century-Crofts, 1957.

I. Education

Carpenter, John R. Role-reversal in the classroom. *Group Psychotherapy,* 1968, *21*(3-4), 155.

Chesler, Mark and Fox, Robert. *Role-playing methods in the classroom.* Chicago: Science Research Associates, 1966. Excellent small booklet, approximately 60 pages as introduction to this method. Available from Science Research Associates, Booklet #13-131, 7200 S. Leamington Avenue, Chicago, Illinois 60638.

Ferinden, W. E. Multidimensional approach in resolving racial tension in the schools utilizing psychodramatic technique. *Group Psychotherapy and Psychodrama,* 1970, *23*(3-4), 91-96.

Kay, Lillian Wald. Role-playing as a teaching aid. *Sociometry,* 1946, *9*(3-4), 263.

Leonard, George. *Education and Ecstacy.* New York: Delacorte Press, 1968. Projects some possibilities for inclusion of role-playing in education. Along with works of Paul Goodman, A. S. Neill, Edgar Freidenberg, John Holt, and others. Points the way to the future of education.

McCarthy, William. Role-playing and teaching. Unpublished masters thesis, Stanford University School of Education, 1959. Good bibliography.

Nichols, Hildred. Role-playing in the primary grades. *Group Psychotherapy,* 1954, *7*(3-4), 238-241.

Shaftel, George and Shaftel, Fannie. *Role-playing for social values.* Englewood Cliffs, New Jersey: Prentice-Hall, 1967. Very good book on applications of role-playing in schoolrooms.

Stanford, Gene and Roark, Albert E. *Human interaction in education.* Boston: Allyn & Bacon, 1973.

Stanford, Gene and Stanford, Barbara D. *Learning skills through games*. New York: Citation Press, 1970.
Way, Brian. *Development through drama*. London: Longman Group Ltd., 1967.
Wells, Cecilia G. Psychodrama and creative counseling in the elementary school. *Group Psychotherapy*, 1962, *15*(3-4), 244-252.

J. Professional training

Facos, James. Group psychotherapy and psychodrama in the college classroom—the application of Moreno techniques to the nursery school trainee. *Group Psychotherapy*, 1965, *18*(3), 162-165.
Fine, Leon J. Action group processes and psychodrama in residency training, in Gene Abroms and Greenfield (Eds.) *The new hospital psychiatry*. New York: Academic Press, 1971.
Goldberg, Naomi and Hyde, Robert. Role-playing in psychiatric training. *Journal of Social Psychology*, 1954, *39*(9), 63-74.
Henderson, H. L. Interview training through role-playing. *Vocational Guidance Quarterly*, 1955, *3*(2), 104-106.
Kalisch, L. Experiments in empathy with nursing students. *Nursing Research*, 1971, *20*, 202-211.
Kelly, H. S. et al. Sociodrama: An action-oriented laboratory for teaching interpersonal relationship skills. *Perspectives in Psychiatric Care*, 1968, *6*, 110-115.
Kneisl, C. R. Increasing interpersonal understanding through sociodrama. *Perspectives In Psychiatric Care*, 1968, *6*, 104-109.
Lippitt, Rosemary and Huchell, Anne. Role-playing for personnel and guidance workers. *Group Psychotherapy*, 1955, *8*(2), 89.
Logan, Daniel L. Action-oriented group therapy as a training method for psychiatric student nurses. *Journal of Psychiatric Nursing*, 1969, *7*(5), 201-206.
Merbaum, M. The use of psychodrama as a method of improving the empathic ability of student nurses. Unpublished masters thesis, University of Kansas City, 1957.
Merchant, F. C. The place of psychodrama in the training of the clinician. *Psychological Bulletin*, 1941, *38*, 13-19.
Starr, Adeline and Fagel, E. Training state hospital personnel through psychodrama and sociometry. *Group Psychotherapy*, 1961, *14*(1-2), 55-61.
Stein, Calvert. Psychodrama for nurses in a general hospital. *Group Psychotherapy*, 1961, *14*, 90-94.
Stripling, Robert. Role-playing in guidance training programs. *Teachers College Record*, 1954, 551423-551429.
Swell, Lila. Role-playing in the context of learning theory in casework teaching. *Education for Social Work*, Spring 1968, 70-76.

Teper, L. Role-playing as a tool in mental health education. *School Health Review,* February 1971, *2,* 31-32.
Underwood, Patricia R. Communication through role-playing. *American Journal of Nursing,* 1971, *71*(6), 1184-1186.
Wide open classroom to teach teachers. *Life,* October 1, 1971, 60-64. Referring to the New School for Behavioral Studies, Grand Forks, North Dakota.

K. Applications in industry

Corsini, Raymond J., Shaw, M. E., and Blake, R. R. *Role-playing in business and industry.* New York: Free Press, 1961. Very good book, with fine annotated bibliography especially related to this field, and many articles not noted in this present bibliography.
Klein, Alvan F. *Role-playing in leadership training and group problem solving.* New York: Association Press, 1959.
Lippitt, Ronald. The psychodrama in leadership training. *Sociometry,* 1943, *6,* 286-292.
Stahl, Gustav. Role-playing in industry. *Group Psychotherapy,* 1958, *6*(3-4), 202-215.
Articles on role-playing can also be found in the following journals: *Personnel Journal, Journal of American Society of Training Directors, Journal of Industrial Training,* and the official publication of the N.T.L., *Journal of Applied Behavioral Science.*

L. Applications in religion

Bobroff, Alvin. Religious psychodrama. *Group Psychotherapy,* 1955, *8*(3-4), 347-350.
Braden, Thomas. *LSD and the search for God,* New York: Bantam Books, 1967.
Braden, Thomas. *The age of aquarius.* Chicago: Quadrangle Books, 1970.
Chase, Philip and Farnham, Beverly. A report on religious psychodrama. *Group Psychotherapy,* 1965, *18*(3), 177.
Clayton, G. Maxwell. Sociodrama in a church group. *Group Psychotherapy and Psychodrama,* 1971, *24*(3-4), 97-100.
Cox, Harvey. In praise of festivity. *Saturday Review,* Oct. 25, 1969.
Cox, Harvey. *The feast of fools.* Cambridge: Harvard University Press, 1969.
Greeley, Andrew M. There's a new-time religion on campus. *New York Times Magazine,* June 1, 1969, 14. Interesting article on movement towards occultism, etc.—modern trends in "post-hippie" youth culture.
Hittson, Helen. Psychodrama in a church counseling program. *Group Psychotherapy and Psychodrama,* 1970, *23*(1-2), 113-117.

Keen, Sam. *To a dancing god*. New York: Harper & Row, 1970.

Moreno, J. L. Experimental theology. *Sociatry,* 1948, *2*(1-2), 93-98.

Moreno, J. L. *The words of the father*. Beacon, New York: Beacon House, 1941. His poetry, written as a young man, expressing his ideas.

Needleman, Jacob. *The new religions*. Garden City, N.Y.: Doubleday and Company, 1970.

Neihardt, John G. *Black Elk speaks*. Lincoln: University of Nebraska Press, 1961.

The quest for survival. *Life,* January 9, 1970, *68*(1), 16-30.

Zacher, A. N. The use of psychodrama in pastoral therapy. *Group Psychotherapy,* 1961, *14*(1-2), 164-168.

M. Penology, community confrontation, and intergroup conflict

Franck, P. Psychodrama offers new vista to parolees. *Journal of Rehabilitation,* May-June 1969, *35,* 28-29.

Korn, Richard. Role reversal, judges and criminals. *Time Magazine,* June 7, 1969.

Lassner, Rudolph. Psychodrama in prison. *Group Psychotherapy,* 1951, *3*(1), 87-89.

O'Connell, Walter. Community confrontations: A challenge to psychotherapeutic practice. *Journal of Individual Psychology,* May 1969, *25,* 38-47.

9

Theoretical Bases of the Use of Psychodramatic Methods

A fundamental premise of the theoretical basis for psychodramatic methods rests on a realistic understanding of the nature of eclecticism in psychotherapy and education. An eclectic approach is not simply a superficial and pragmatic dilettantism; rather, it is based on the recognition that each client has a unique set of challenges and abilities. The current research on the varieties of cognitive styles, temperament, educational background, and levels of organizational stress in a system, reaffirms the maxim, "different folks need different strokes."

Psychodramatic methods are to be viewed most realistically as functioning *within* an eclectic approach to the helping relationship. There are moments in any therapy for analysis, individual study, reflection, and careful planning; but at other times, human development demands a level of personal creativity which can best be achieved within a context of spontaneity, active participation, group support, and the freedom to explore many different facets of a situation.

It is the purpose of this chapter to note *how* psychodramatic methods can facilitate the development of human potentialities in psychotherapy and education. Three major avenues of reasoning will be used: (1) that psychodramatic methods can be helpful in the process of emotional problem-solving; (2) that the sense of self can be strengthened effectively by building a wider role repertoire using psychodramatic methods, and (3) that psychodramatic methods are consistent with and capable of being easily integrated with other psychotherapeutic methods.

EMOTIONAL PROBLEM-SOLVING

Many of the decisions which we face daily require some consideration of the nonrational factors in our lives. Skills of introspection are needed in order to properly weigh and include the emotional dimensions of any situation. In order to gain a perspective on the unconscious determinants of one's choices, it is necessary to find ways of developing insight into interpersonal relationships. The use of psychodramatic methods can complement verbal methods in facilitating *the analysis of* the many different dimensions of emotional problem-solving. The process of psychotherapy or education about feelings thus can be viewed in terms of: (1) establishing a context which maximizes the conditions for personal growth and (2) partially analyzing the modes of problem-solving.

THE CONTEXT OF GROWTH

One of the most fundamental principles of any form of psychotherapy is the establishment of a healthy helping relationship. So much of what transpires in this context is based on the factor of *suggestion,* which, in turn, is affected by role-behavior of the helper, the expectation of help, and by the client's acceptance of his own role as the one who is to be helped. The presence of others who share the client's belief in the healing system (e.g., in group setting) heightens the effectiveness of the suggestion factors of psychotherapy. The director who uses psychodramatic methods increases these suggestion factors by his active self-disclosure, and his skillful use of the dramatic dimensions of his approach.

A second psychotherapeutic factor begins to operate when the director establishes norms for the group: acceptance, permissiveness, honesty, self-observation, expectations of risk-taking, expression of emotion, self-disclosure, discussion, mutuality, and so forth. In psychodrama the director *models* these behaviors, as well as talks *about* them. The group process then functions on a fail-safe basis; the level of judgment by peers is reduced, and support for creativity and spontaneity is reinforced.

A further factor of therapy is the use of a specified time in a setting of sufficient length for each person to get involved. The use of psychodramatic methods demands more time than other approaches, because it recognizes the role of the warm-up. Time for warming up to the point of creativity and spontaneity is necessary in order to reach a level of emotional expression (catharsis) that will produce insight. The usefulness of time-extended factors has been noted in the work of "Marathon Group Therapy" and weekend workshops for personal growth. (See References, Chapter 10, under Mintz, Stoller, and Bach.)

The last point in establishing a context for growth is the use of individual-centered format. Dealing with the problems of one protagonist at a time within the group setting has several advantages over the group-centered approach, in which the director deals primarily with issues of total group process. In the individual-centered approach, the protagonist presents a concrete example of a problem which is often representative of the group theme at the time; enactment helps to go beyond abstract discussion into the deeper feelings relating to a problem. The director then uses the group to facilitate the protagonist's emotional problem-solving in several ways: as a source of confrontation, support, consensual feedback, concern, and reinforcement of the protagonist's adaptive behaviors. Certainly the attention of the group increases the factors of positive concern and expectation (i.e., suggestion) for the protagonist's growth processes.

CLARIFICATION OF THE PROBLEM

Whether or not a group is used, the process of exploring and integrating the emotional dimensions of any problem is facilitated in many ways by using psychodramatic methods.

First of all, when the problem is presented, an enactment can help to bring out the *concrete behavior* which is involved. So many protagonists tend to habitually explain, intellectualize, or be defensively vague or circumstantial; concrete presentation circumvents these defenses. "Diagnosis," (i.e., seeing-through) is most effective when the director discovers some of the dimensions of the situation which the protagonist might ignore or avoid in a verbal narrative. Recreating the event in an enactment can help the protagonist to stop explaining and just show what happened.

Once the situation is presented concretely in an enactment it usually becomes obvious to the observer that the protagonist is engaging in and/or reacting to nonverbal communications, many of which he is only dimly aware of. Using psychodramatic methods, the director helps the protagonist to become explicitly aware of these gestures, expressions, and postures. Incongruities between verbal and nonverbal communications often account for a major portion of the difficulties encountered in interpersonal relationships. For example, a mother's statement to her children, "Go ahead and have a good time—don't worry about me," if accompanied by a pained expression usually evokes a response of feeling guilty and worrying about mother. Furthermore, the exploration of the meanings of the protagonist's own nonverbal communication can become an avenue for self-confrontation of character defenses—an essential step towards insight (see Chapter 5). There are many other action methods which can be utilized to help the protagonist to view his own behavior more objectively, as well as to think about the impact that the behavior has on others.

Thirdly, psychodramatic methods rapidly move the protagonist into the emotional levels of his problem. Through dramatization, the use of supportive doubling, and the judicious use of physical contact in an enactment, the protagonist *experiences* the feelings as well as talks about them. Of course, the use of touching, whether it be in holding, patting, or shoving, must be carefully applied for it is a very powerful avenue to the evocation of emotion. Yet, if the director is skillful and works in a mutual relationship with the protagonist, he can greatly extend the effectiveness of the participatory learning experience.

The many methods noted in Chapters 4, 5, and 6 can help the protagonist not only to discuss, but also to actively *experience* the issues at hand, which is the whole point of participatory and experiential education.

Fourthly, the process of emotional problem-solving requires consideration not only of the protagonist's feelings, but of the feelings of the others with whom he is interacting. The development of an *empathic understanding* can be facilitated by actually having the protagonist enact the role of the other person. Through role reversal, the protagonist discovers many viewpoints which expand his own insight and help him to choose more adaptive responses.

Finally, the discussion as to possible solutions in problem-solving can be extended into active working through; not only are the new ideas talked about, but by using psychodramatic methods, they *are tried out in a simulated situation*. The group members can then *model* the behaviors they suggest. Successful and spontaneous behaviors are reinforced, while ineffective adaptations become immediately apparent and are gradually extinguished. The group's tolerant support provides a corrective emotional experience. All of these components of working through are made more vivid through adding psychodramatic to the verbal-analytic methods.

FUNCTION OF SURPLUS REALITY

If the use of psychodramatic methods in dealing with emotional problem-solving seems "artificial" or "gimmicky," it may be due to a common misunderstanding as to the role of *surplus reality* in our lives. The view of man as *only* existentially being-in-the-world, with one unified "core" of authenticity, denies the phenomenon of imagination. It is our imagination which accounts for the self-reflective dimensions of our consciousness, the ability to see ourselves at a distance. Man is the only animal who becomes embarrassed, who considers his own death, who does not learn from experience (because he clings to his illusions). These aspects of our essential humanity are manifestations of the imagination.

The imagination represents that dimension of our lives which is our *surplus reality*. We are kings, we are slaves; we are again children, we exist ten years in the future. The invitation to utilize our imagination, to say, "if . . ," is the essence of play, hypnosis, and psychodrama.

I maintain that the willingness to suspend disbelief in order to permit a period of fantasy is not artificial. Nor, when explicitly chosen, is the involvement in imagination a regressive function. Indeed, the modality of play is a powerful and, at times essential vehicle to (1) provide some distance and ego-protection, (2) change attitudinal set, (3) function as an intermediary between the polarities of fully committed action and passive reflection; subjectivity and objectivity; the esthetic and the pragmatic; spontaneity and calculation, etc.; and (4) especially, through use of imagery, play serves as an avenue for entrance into the complex world of feelings, mythologic complexes, and spiritual dimensions.

The use of psychodramatic techniques is thus becoming an important approach for the use of imagination as a synthetic function in personal development.

EXPANSION OF THE ROLE-REPERTOIRE

A second major argument for the use of psychodramatic methods rests on the basis not of psychodynamic theory, but of *role* theory. The view of man as evolving along many simultaneous dimensions is a basic premise. Furthermore, psychopathology reflects not only a distortion of one of these aspects of personality, but often represents a compensatory expression of one facet of the personality primarily due to a lack of development of another. For example, a person with few opportunities, or validation for building skills in the realm of imagination and feelings, tends to become over-intellectualized. His intellectualization is a "vacuum activity," (a term borrowed from ethology, referring to the time-filling behavior of animals when their normal outlets are frustrated, such as by being in a cage.)

Psychotherapy and education viewed from the position of role theory would emphasize the training of the person's capacity in a variety of roles which can balance and complement each other. The normal function of play in childhood is to at least symbolically enact a wide variety of roles which then become a core of identifications and ego-strengths. For example, the child must play at being a mother before he or she can convert internalized nurturing behaviors given to him by his parents into an active sense of nurturing others.

A full presentation of the importance of role theory would take more than one book. Suffice it to say that I believe it is necessary for people to build a wide role-repertoire, including a variety of forms of skills (see Table 1, p. 111).

The use of psychodramatic methods can be an effective form of *engaging* in learning about these many roles, rather than simply talking about them. Psychodramatic role-playing is a major form of *experiential* and *participatory* education, and education is a major aspect of a total psychotherapeutic program.

Some specific ways in which developing a wider role-repertoire may function are:

1. *the sense of choice* is increased as there are more behavioral roles with which one is familiar.

2. *the importance of many different aspects of life* is validated through role-taking behaviors: dimensions such as play, dance, achievement, competition, imagination.

3. *identification*   The practice in taking other roles builds an increased capacity for empathy. Meerloo writes, "Partaking in the psyche of the other means using the vicarious signs of preverbal communication. Moreno, the founder of modern group therapy, calls this mutual partaking and emotional communicative understanding from afar 'telic sensitivity' and 'telic-reciprocity.''

4. *experiencing the sense of self*   Taking active and creatively spontaneous role behaviors in many dimensions fulfills an extremely important function: that of validating the sense of one's own vitality, will, authenticity, feelings, imagery, and, in short, the sense of being deeply alive, of being a "self."

5. *flexibility*   Role-taking behavior, if reinforced, helps the individual to allow himself to develop a sense of mastery in many different role situations: father, lover, son, judge, student, friend, teacher, policeman. In turn, the components of each role can be applied more easily in new situations where syntheses must be developed. In other words, the more media an artist can competently master, the more he is able to "break set" and create new forms out of the traditional methods.

INTEGRATION WITH OTHER PSYCHO-THERAPEUTIC APPROACHES

Within the general framework of eclecticism as noted at the beginning of this chapter, I consider the various theoretical systems of psychotherapy, and their practical methodologies as being essentially compatible with each other. Each approach relates best to only a few facets of human experience, and a flexible application of several different methods may be required in the individualized treatment of each case. Moreover, the synthesis of two methods often can result in significantly greater effectiveness than could be obtained from either method being used alone.

For example, the psychodynamics of the Oedipal conflict as described by psychoanalytic theory may often emerge spontaneously within a psychodrama. This phenomenon is capitalized upon by some orthodox psychoanalysts in France, who use several therapists in creating psychodrama for selected patients. The interactional dynamics as described by Sullivan, Adler, and Eric Berne can often be illustrated to a family or group by recreating the conflict situations in a psychodramatic enactment.

The theoretical concepts relating to ego-splitting, (in object-relations theory), complexes (in Jungian theory) and autonomous body language (in Gestalt therapy) all can be made more demonstrable by objectifying parts of the person's psyche in psychodramatic enactment. The conflicting facets of the personality are then helped to symbolically "encounter" each other in an effort to reach a constructive re-synthesis of the personality.

Other therapeutic systems which have much in common with the psychodramatic method include George Kelly's *role prescriptions* in his *Theory of Personal Constructs;* the system of *Direct Analysis* as practiced by John Rosen; and the ritualized activities of traditional practitioners of non-Western medicine in other cultures.

Harold Greenwald, in his book *Active Psychotherapy,* reviews many of the other active approaches which have become more relevant in the last decade. The need for a variety of pragmatic, brief therapies has become obvious as the field of mental health has begun to accept the challenge of varying personality problems in our culture.

In addition to therapies which are dramatic in their quality, there are also many approaches which utilize subtler aspects of role-playing or other psychodramatic techniques. The techniques of assertion training in the behavior therapies; and of "side-taking" in conjoint family therapy are both essentially psycho-dramatic in their process. In addition, psychodramatic methods are frequently being used as an integral part of many therapy or human potential groups which use transactional analysis, reality therapy, psychosynthesis, or bioenergetics as their main orientation. Indeed, I am aware of professionals in almost every facet of education, organizational development, and psychotherapy who have been able to creatively adapt psychodramatic methods to the requirements of their tasks.

SUMMARY

The theoretical basis of the use of psychodramatic methods rests on a foundation of eclecticism in the choice of psychotherapeutic and educational approaches. Psychodramatic methods may be more specifically applied for two purposes: analysis and synthesis. As an analytic agent, psychodrama can be invaluable in clarifying the person's dynamics at every stage in the process of emotional problem-solving. In the task of ego-synthesis, psychodramatic methods may be applied to facilitate the development of a widened repertoire and as an aid in generating skills for using the imagination. Finally, by enabling the participants to engage in trial behaviors within a fail-safe context, symbolic ventilation and reinforcement of new learning can occur.

Many of the contemporary psychotherapies utilize a combination of analytic and synthesizing processes. Most of these approaches may become even more effective through the use of psychodramatic methods, either as an adjunct or as an integral component of their therapeutic practice.

References

Abroms, Gene. The new eclecticism. *Archives of General Psychiatry,* May 1969, *20,* 513-523.

Ackerman, Nathan. Comparisons of group psychotherapy and psychoanalysis. *Group Psychotherapy,* 1951, *3*(3-4), 212-216.

Allerhand, Melvin. A comparison of two approaches to group psychotherapy and psychodrama. *Group Psychotherapy,* 1953, *5*(4), 199-204.

Allport, Gordon W. The fruits of eclecticism, bitter or sweet? in *The person in psychology: Selected essays.* Boston: Beacon Press, 1968.

Biddle, Bruce J. and Thomas, Edwin J. *Role theory: Concepts and research.* New York: John Wiley, 1966. This thorough text has good reviews and theoretical correlations for the use of role-playing.

Bischof, Ledford J. *Interpreting personality theories.* New York: Harper & Row, 1964. Has a chapter on some theoretical aspects of Moreno's theories. One of the few commentators on theory I have found. Complete bibliography of Moreno's writings up to 1961.

Blatner, Howard A. Theoretical aspects of psychodrama—General comments. *Bulletin de Psychologie,* 1969-70, *23*(285), 13-16.

Deikman, Arthur. Bimodal consciousness. *Archives of General Psychiatry.* 1971, *25*(6), 481-489.

Ehrenwald, J. *Psychotherapy: Myth and method.* New York: Grune and Stratton, 1966.

Elm, Alan C. (Ed.) *Role-playing, reward and attitude change.* New York: Van Nostrand Insight, 1969. Psychological studies regarding effectiveness of role-playing.

Erkison, Erik H. Toys and reasons (the function of play), in Mary Haworth (Ed.) *Child psychotherapy–Practice and theory.* New York: Basic Books, 1964.

Fingarette, Herbert. *The self in transformation.* New York: Basic Books, 1963.

Forer, B. The taboo against touching in psychotherapy. *Psychotherapy: Theory, Research and Practice,* 1969, *6*(V), 225-231.

Glasser, William. The civilized identity society: Mankind enters phase four. *Saturday Review,* 1972, *55*(8), 26-33.

Goldstein, Arnold P. and Simonson, Norman R. Social psychological approaches to psychotherapy research, in A. S. Bergen and Sol L. Garfield (Eds.) *Handbook of psychotherapy and behavior change.* New York: John Wiley, 1971.

Gosnell, D. Some similarities and dissimilarities between the psychodramaturgical approaches of J. L. Moreno and Erving Goffman. *International Journal of Sociometry and Sociatry,* 1964, *3*, 94.

Huizinga, Johann. *Homo Ludens: A study of the play element in culture.* Boston: Beacon Press, 1966. Basic theory, very creative ideas, which I feel are consistent and complementary to Moreno's theories and, indeed, to any theory of personality.

Janis, D. and King, B. Influence of role-playing in opinion change. *Journal of Abnormal and Social Psychology,* 1954, *49*, 211-218.

Jennings, Helen H. Leadership and sociometric choice, in E. Maccoby, T. Newcomb, and E. Hartley (Eds.) *Readings in social psychology* (3rd ed.) New York: Holt, Rinehart & Winston, 1958.

Kipper, David A. On spontaneity. *Group Psychotherapy,* March 1967, *20*(1).

Kreitler, Hans and Eblinger, S. Validation of psychodramatic behavior against behavior in life. *British Journal of Medical Psychology,* 1968, *41,* 185.

Lakin, Martin and Carsun, Robert C. A therapeutic vehicle in search of a theory of therapy. *Journal of Applied Behavioral Science,* 1966, *2*(1), 27-40.

Mann, John H. Experimental evaluations of role-playing. *Psychology Bulletin,* 1956, *53,* 227-234.

Mann, John H. and Mann, Carol H. Role-play experience and interpersonal adjustment. *Journal of Counseling Psychology,* 1959, *6,* 148-152.

Marmor, Judd. The nature of the psychotherapeutic process, in G. Usden (Ed.) *Psychoneurosis and schizophrenia.* Philadelphia: J. B. Lippincott, 1966.

Meerloo, Joost A. M. Why do we sympathize with each other? *Archives of General Psychiatry,* October 1966, *15,* 390-397.

Mintz, Elizabeth. On the rationale of touch in psychotherapy. *Psychotherapy: Theory, Research and Practice,* 1969, *6*(4), 232-235.

Ortman, Harriet. How psychodrama fosters creativity. *Group Psychotherapy,* 1966, *19*(3-4), 201.

Patterson, C. H. Diversion and convergence in psychotherapy. *American Journal of Psychotherapy,* 1967, *21*(1), 4-17.

Perls, Frederick S. Workshop vs individual therapy. *Journal of Long Island Consultation Center,* 1967, *5*(2), 13-17.

Sarbin, Theodore R. The concept of role-taking. *Sociometry,* August 1943, *6,* 273.

Shapiro, Stewart. The selves inside you. *Explorations Magazine,* May 1966, *6,* 3-18.

Spiegelman, Marvin and Klopfer, B. Some dimensions of psychotherapy, in C. A. Meier (Ed.) *Spectrum psychologie.* Zurich: Rasher & Co., 1965.

Sturm, I. E. An attempt to dramatize the double-bind hypothesis of the schizophrenic family. *Journal of Psychology,* January 1971, *77,* 55-66.

Sturm, I. E. A behavioral outline of psychodrama. *Psychotherapy: Theory, Research and Practice,* 1970, *7*(4), 245-247.

Torrey, E. Fuller. What western psychotherapists can learn from witch doctors. *American Journal of Orthopsychiatry,* 1972, *42*(1), 69-76.

Wagner, M. K. Reinforcement of the expression of anger through role-playing. *Behavioral Research and Therapy,* February 1968, *6,* 91-95.

Yalom, Irvin. *Theory and practice of group psychotherapy.* New York: Basic Books, 1970.

10

The Training of the Psycho-dramatist

The challenge of using psychodramatic methods demands much more than the knowledge of many techniques. The subject of the director's attention is the fragile world of personal emotions, and working with people in this way demands a sense of professionalism that is beyond the role of a technician. Indeed, the professional who would become a director of psychodrama must use *himself* as a major vehicle for his method, which is tantamount in many ways to describing the commitment of the artist. I believe the teacher or psychotherapist who uses psychodramatic methods should build his skills in three interdependent areas: (1) his knowlege of his methods, principles, and techniques; (2) his understanding of personality theory and its relation to an evolving philosophy of life; and (3) his own personal development and maturity.

In this chapter I will describe my recommendations for the training of the psychodramatist. I believe the future director should work along several simultaneous lines, which will be noted below.

TRAINING IN PSYCHODRAMA

The student of psychodrama must first have some experience in being involved in many psychodramas led by others, and must play the roles of auxiliary ego, double, and, most importantly, the protagonist. Furthermore, the student should begin to direct small enactments, situation-tests, or circumscribed role-playing activities *under supervision* as soon as he can. Of course, this demands a great deal of risk-taking, but it is only through *experiential* learning that a director can learn his field. In other words, the model of training for psychodrama is most similar to an apprenticeship, in which a student assumes gradually increasing responsibilities under close observation and feedback from one more experienced than he.

Furthermore, the student should experience a wide variety of roles within different contexts; role-taking skills can be built through adult "play" in theater games, guided fantasy, story telling, and creative dramatics. Spontaneity training activities may be very valuable in this regard.

THE MORENO INSTITUTE

The major center for training in and information about psychodrama is the Moreno Institute. The institute at the Beacon Sanitarium is located about sixty miles north of New York on the banks of the Hudson River. The hospital there has been converted into a residential center, where one may attend training workshops for one or several weeks. There is also an institute in New York City where one may attend open sessions almost every night.

Information regarding training sessions and annual conventions of the International or American Societies for Group Psychotherapy and Psychodrama may be obtained by writing to the Moreno Institute, or by subscribing to the official journal of the Society, *Group Psychotherapy and Psychodrama*.

In addition, one can send for many of Dr. Moreno's books, some back issues of the journals, and notifications of lecture-demonstrations which may be forthcoming in this area. The addresses are:

> World Center for Psychodrama, Sociometry, and
> Group Psychotherapy (Moreno Academy)
> P O Box 311, 259 Wolcott Avenue
> Beacon, New York 12508

> New York Institute of Psychodrama
> 236 W. 78th Street
> New York 10024

Other Institutes:

The Institute for Sociotherapy
(Dr. and Mrs. Robert Siroka)
39 E. 20th Street
New York, N. Y. 10003

St. Elizabeth's Hospital
Psychodrama Unit
(Mr. James Enneis)
Washington, D. C. 20037

St. Louis State Hospital
Training Institute of Psychodrama
5400 Arsenal Street
St. Louis, Missouri 63139

Evergreen Institute
Psychodrama Training Workshops
(Carl Hollander)
3831 W. Wagon Trail Drive
Littleton, Colorado 80120

Role Training Associates of California
(Martin Haskell, Ph.D.)
1290 E. Ocean Boulevard
Long Beach, California 90802

San Francisco Psychotherapy and Psychodrama Institute (Thomas E. McCormick, M.D. and Adele Deeths McCormick)
364—14th. Avenue
San Francisco, California 94118

Seminars in Group Process
(Leon Fine, Ph.D.)
7433 Garden Home Road
Portland, Oregon 97223

International Foundation for Human Relations
(Dr. Dean Elefthery, President, Miami, Florida
Dr. Dolf Grunwald, Secretary)
Nic Maesstraat 20, Amsterdam, Netherlands

There are also many other directors and trained professionals who do not at present offer a formal regular training program. In addition, there may be some programs that I do not know about. An attempt at a comprehensive listing would be fruitless at this time. The interested reader can write to one of the above addresses regarding programs in his area.

PERSONAL DEVELOPMENT

The person who plans to develop his skills as a director of psychodrama must pursue his own personal development with the same commitment that he gives to his professional training. The psychodramatist, like the true psychotherapist or teacher, is an artist in that he must synthesize what he knows with who he is. Authenticity, spontaneity, and intuition must be interwoven with experience, some talent, and rigorous self-disciplined study and introspection.

I think that the director who is in training should subject himself to a course of individual psychotherapy, if he can find a therapist with whom he feels a bond of rapport. Group therapy or encounter group experiences can be valuable adjuncts to a therapy experience. If one rejects the idea of therapy, one should at least establish a continuing professional consultation relationship, one which explores the student-director's personal feelings, counter-transferences, and blind spots. The director will be able to help others only in areas where he has himself achieved some clear vision.

RELATED AREAS

The director should develop his knowledge of many related areas. Any of the studies in the behavioral sciences can be quite useful to the student of psychodrama. Subjects such as ethology, sociology, comparative religion, political science, and other related areas are quite productive. Some of the main fields of study which are *essential* to the development of the psychodramatist are noted below. References on some of these fields will be noted at the end of the chapter.

Group Process   The insights derived from work in group psychotherapy and small group research in social psychology are an especially important keystone for the work of any director. Readings in the professional texts and journals are strongly recommended.

General Psychology   A director *must* have some frameworks of personality theory within which he can operate. Psychodynamic, sociocultural, interactional, developmental, and existential theories can complement each other. The study in this field should be continuous throughout the director's professional life.

Humanistic Psychology   This vitally important field has been called the "third force" in contemporary American psychology (psychoanalytically-oriented and behavioral approaches being the first two "forces"). Humanistic psychology has a number of concepts and values which are most relevant to the high-intensity technologic environment and the issues of identity-confusion which are so prevalent in modern society. The writing of the humanistic psychologists have become the theoretical backbone of the human potential movement. The writings of Gordon Allport, James F. T. Bugental, Victor Frankl, A. H. Maslow, Sidney Jourard, Rollo May, Gardner Murphy, Clark Moustakis, and many other therapists and philosophers are most relevant for the director of psychodrama.

Futurology   A significant portion of the problems in America today are related to the fact that values, culture, and technologies are rapidly changing. The stresses in contemporary families, for example, are often related to the evolving concepts of the nature of marital or filial relationships. Therefore, the dramatist who will be helping with such issues should develop some perspective on the changes in society today.

Communication theory   Another increasingly relevant field of investigation relates to the applications of communication theory in psychotherapy, family dynamics, organizational systems, and small group process. It is an invaluable aid to the director of psychodrama to understand some of the ways that people confuse and mystify each other in their patterns of interaction.

Nonverbal communication   A major dimension of communications theory which is especially valuable to a director is an awareness of the many facets and powerful effects of nonverbal communications. Issues of kinesics, proxemics (territoriality), mannerisms of speech and gesture, the impact of tone, rhythm and inflection in voice, can all be applied in a psychodrama to clarify the dynamics of the interaction.

The Human Potential movement   The cultural phenomena of encounter groups, sensitivity training, growth centers, and many other related forms of education often utilize a great deal of psychodramatic methods in their small group work. The task of facilitation of a sensitivity training group is very similar to the task of directing psychodrama, and the two roles have much overlap in skills and practice; thus the director should be well acquainted with the field of encounter groups in order to learn from the best that is there and to avoid the most common abuses.

OTHER ACTION APPROACHES IN PSYCHOTHERAPY

A host of innovations have been introduced in the field of education and psychotherapy. The director should also be eclectic enough to interweave a variety of these innovations, along with the use of psychodramatic methods, into his work with groups. Some of the more important approaches are Gestalt therapy, guided fantasy and psychosynthesis, bioenergetics and the use of body movement, sensory awakening and massage methods, the use of the time-extended (marathon) motif, and the application of creative media to the developmental process. I strongly recommend the student's reading the related literature noted in the references at the end of the chapter.

SUMMARY

The committed student of psychotherapy who wishes to integrate the use of psychodramatic methods as part of his armamentarium takes on the responsibility of understanding a powerful approach to working with other people's feelings. He himself should develop along the lines of personal growth, acquisition of knowledge about his subject matter and media, and the construction of some philosophy of the nature of the helping relationship. This chapter has noted some of the dimensions which I have found to be especially helpful as complements to my skills in working with psychodramatic methods.

References

Assagioli, Robert, *Psychosynthesis*. New York: Hobbs-Dorman, 1965. Extensive and eclectic view of psychotherapy, adaptable especially for open-ended "growth."

Association of humanistic psychology newsletter. San Francisco. Related to human potential movement. Address: Association of Humanistic Psychology, 416 Hoffman Street, San Francisco, California 94114.

Bach, George R. *Intensive group psychotherapy*. New York: Ronald Press, 1956.

Bach, George R. The marathon group (part 1). *Psychological Reports*, 1966, *18*, 995-1002. Part II, 1967, *20*, 995-999. Part III, 1967, *20*, 1147-1158.

Bach, George R. and Wyden, Peter. *The intimate enemy: How to fight fair in love and marriage*. New York: Avon Paperbacks, 1969. Good introduction to dynamics of confrontation. Very valuable reading, good notes.

Birdwhistell, Ray L. *Kinesics and context—Essays on body motion communication*. Philadelphia: University of Pennsylvania Press, 1970.

Blank, Leonard, Gottsagen, G. B., and Gottsagen, M. C. *Confrontation: Encounters in self and interpersonal awareness*. New York: Macmillan Company, 1971.

Boies, Karen G. Role playing as a behavior change technique: Review of the empirical literature *Psychotherapy: Theory, Research and Practice*, 1972, *9*(2), 185-192.

Burton, Arthur (Ed.) *Encounter: The theory and practice of encounter groups*. San Francisco: Jossey-Bass, Inc., 1970. Fair group of articles, but almost no references.

Egan, Gerard. *Encounter: Group processes for interpersonal growth*. Belmont, California: Brooks/Cole, 1970. Extensive and scholarly.

Fagan, Joen (Ed.) *Gestalt therapy now*. Palo Alto, California: Science and Behavior Books, 1970. Excellent book with many articles relating to this method. Also available in paperback from Harper & Row, New York.

Fast, Julius. *Body languange*. New York: M. Evans & Co., 1970.

Feldman, Somdor S. *Mannerisms of speech and gesture in everyday life*. New York: International Universities Press, 1959.

Fine, Leon J. Nonverbal aspects of psychodrama, in J. Masserman and J. L. Moreno (Eds.) *Social psychotherapy*, Volume 4 of *Progress in psychotherapy*. New York: Grune and Stratton, 1959.

Gendzel, Ivan B. Marathon group therapy: Rationale and techniques, in Jules Masserman (Ed.) *Current psychiatric therapies*, Vol. 12. New York: Grune and Stratton, 1972.

Goble, Frank G. *The third force: The psychology of Abraham Maslow*. New York: Grossman Publishers, 1970. Reviews other works.

Goldberg, Carl. *Encounter*, New York: Science House, 1971.

Golembiewski, R. T. and Blumberg, Arthur (Eds.) *Sensitivity training and the laboratory approach*. Itasca, Illinois: F. E. Peacock Publications, 1970.

Gottschalk, L. A. and Davidson, R. Sensitivity groups, encounter groups, training groups, and marathon groups, in H. I. Kaplan and B. J. Sadock (Eds.) *Comprehensive group psychotherapy*. Baltimore: Williams & Wilkins, 1971.

Gunther, Bernard. *Sense relaxation–Below your mind. (A book of experiments in being alive.)* New York: Collier Books, 1968. Picture book of sensory awareness exercises, for individuals, dyads, groups.

Gunther, Bernard and Fusco, Paul. *What to do 'till the Messiah comes*. New York: Collier Books, 1970.

Gustaitis, Rasa. *Turning on*. London: Weidenfeld & Nicolson, 1969. A good current overview of the various growth center activities, including chapters on Esalen, "joy workshops," Zen, and other approaches. Recommended.

Haley, Jay. *Strategies of psychotherapy*. New York: Grune and Stratton, 1963.

Hammer, Max. The directed daydream technique. *Psychotherapy: Theory, Research and Practice*, 1967, *4*(4), 173.

Lakin, Martin. *Interpersonal encounter: Theory and practice in sensitivity training*. New York: McGraw-Hill, 1972.

Leuner, Hans Carl. Guided affective imagery. *American Journal of Psychotherapy*. 1969, *23*(1), 4-22. Significant tool, also called *guided fantasy*.

Lowen, Alexander. *Pleasure: A creative approach to life*. New York: Coward-McCann, 1970. Latest book in bioenergetic exercises and philosophy.

Mintz, Elizabeth E. *Marathon groups: Symbol and reality*. New York: Appleton-Century-Crofts, 1971. Excellent and scholarly.

Otto, H. A. (Ed.) *Explorations in human potentialities*. Springfield, Ill.: Charles C Thomas, 1966. Significant book on directions of growth movement with articles by Perls, Selver, Mogar, and others.

Otto, H. A. and Mann, John (Eds.) *Ways of growth: Approaches to expanding awareness*. New York: Grossman Publishers, 1968. An interesting variety of methods by many authors active in human potential movement. Recommended.

Pesso, Albert. *Movement in psychotherapy: Psychomotor techniques and training*. New York: New York University Press, 1969. An excellent book on many methods which have a blending of psychodramatic techniques, dance, and movement therapy, and other action approaches. He is coming out with another book soon.

Peterson, Severin. *A catalogue of ways people grow*, Vol. 1. New York: Ballantine Books, 1971.

Rogers, Carl *Carl Rogers on encounter groups*. New York: Harper & Row, 1971.

Rogers, Carl, and Stevens, Barry, *Person to person: The problem of being human*. Lafayette, California: Real People Press, 1969. The best first reading to introduce the novice into the basic ideas of humanistic psychology, which underlies most of the goals and norms of encounter groups. *Strongly recommended*. Also available in paperback from Pocket Books, New York.

Rolf, Ida. *Structural integration*. San Francisco: Guild for Structural Integration, 1969.

Scheflen, Albert E. *Body language and the social order*. Englewood Cliffs, New Jersey: Prentice-Hall, 1972.

Schutz, William C. *Here comes everybody*. New York: Harper & Row, 1971. This is one of the best introductions to the encounter group culture.

Siroka, Robert W., Siroka, E., and Schloss, G. (Eds.) *Sensitivity training and group encounters*. New York: Grosset & Dunlap, 1971. One of the best introductions to encounter groups.

Solomon, Lawrence and Berzon, Betty (Eds.) *New perspectives in encounter groups*. San Francisco: Jossey-Bass Inc., 1972.

Stoller, Frederick H. Marathon group therapy, in George Gazda (Ed.) *Innovations in group psychotherapy*. Springfield, Ill.: Charles C Thomas, 1968. Good review of use of marathon methods.

Sutich, A. J. and Vich, M. *Readings in humanistic psychology*. New York: Free Press, 1969.

Brief History of Psychodrama

A BIOGRAPHY OF J. L. MORENO, M.D.

The history of the development of psychodrama is essentially equivalent to the biography of one man, Dr. Jacob Levy Moreno. His story would easily fill an entire book; here, I will note some of the highlights of his eventful life.

Jacob Levy Moreno was born on May 19, 1892, in Bucharest, Rumania, and five years later his family moved to Vienna. Moreno became a student of philosophy at the University of Vienna (1910-1912), and from his earliest years was interested in the theological and religious dimensions of creativity and spontaneity. In 1911, Moreno observed and began to catalyze the play of children in the Vienna Gardens. Here was the germination of psychodrama and improvisatory dramatics.

While in medical school, Moreno became involved with a form of social action: the challenge of helping the alienated class of prostitutes in Vienna. With other physicians, he initiated small self-help groups; this work marked the beginnings of group psychotherapy, as well as being one of the earliest examples of practical community psychiatry.

After receiving his medical degree from the University of Vienna in 1917, he worked at a refugee damp in Mittendorf. There, he began to attempt some scientific research with the cultural and group dynamics of the refugee population.

During the years 1914-1921, Moreno continued his creative activities in the realm of poetry, philosophy, theology, and literature. He edited a literary journal, *Daimon,* and associated with many of the intellectuals of Vienna at that time, such as Martin Buber and Max Scheler. However his philosophy was closely related to interpersonal themes. Terms such as "here-and-now" and "encounter," so popular today in the human potential movement, were to be found as key ideas in Moreno's poetic writings of this early period. One of the best known of these works is his book, *The Words of the Father*.

The years 1921-1923 saw the birth of "the Theater of Spontaneity" (das Stegreif Theater). Issues of current events ("the Living Newspaper") were subjects of the theater's activities at first, but later Moreno applied this improvisatory setting to the treatment of individuals, marriages, and small groups. It is of interest that the idea of psychodrama followed, rather than preceded, Moreno's work in religion, group psychotherapy, and sociometry.

In 1925, Dr. Moreno moved to the United States in order to find a more fertile field for his explorations. He lived in New York City and applied his methods to the challenges of emotionally disturbed hospitalized children, prisons, and sociopolitical psychology ("the Impromptu Theater"). His use of recording devices in the process of evaluating psychotherapy methods was, at that time, the first application of this technique. Later, when television was developed, Dr. Moreno was the first to note many of its therapeutic possibilities also.

During the next several years, Dr. Moreno developed his ideas in many directions. While working at residential treatment centers for adolescents, he further elaborated on the work that began at Mittendorf, culminating in his book *Who Shall Survive?—Foundations of Sociometry, Group Psychotherapy, and Sociodrama*. (Sociometry has become a major tool in sociology today.) Moreno also emphasized the value of work with groups, and in 1932 coined the term *group psychotherapy*. He thus became a major force in the introduction of new ideas into the field of American psychiatry.

In 1936, the Moreno Sanitarium was established in Beacon, New York, and became a school, a hospital, and the first real theater of psychodrama, as well as his home. In 1937, he edited and published his first journal, *Sociometry*. Over the next several years he continued his work in many interdisciplinary fields: social psychology, psychotherapy, sociology, and philosophy, among others. Many of those who would later become prominent in various fields were associated with Dr. Moreno in this early period—Kurt Lewin, Gardner Murphy, Ronald Lippitt, Leland Bradford, Kenneth Benne, Jack Gibb. (The last three were later to become founders of the "T-Group"—The National Training Laboratories (N.T.L.)—which, in turn, was to become a cornerstone of the human potential movement.)

During the Second World War, Dr. Moreno advised the military services in the applications of role-playing to personnel selection and management. He was also influential in the growth of group psychotherapy as a treatment modality in military and veterans hospitals.

After the war, Moreno continued to publish monographs, books, and a number of articles (see bibliography). He married Zerka Toeman in 1949, and together they began a routine of international conferences and travels, lecture-demonstrations, and prolific writing, which has continued to the present time. Moreno's influence can be found in many of the innovations in psychiatry over the last generation: e.g., family therapy, therapeutic community, Gestalt therapy, and many others.

In summary, the development of psychodrama should be viewed as inextricably interwoven with Moreno's work in philosophy, group psychotherapy, sociology, personality theory, and social psychiatry. Some of the concepts which he emphasized fifty years ago have only recently become recognized as vitally relevant for the challenges of the modern world (see Table 2). Throughout his life, Dr. Moreno has not only maintained an energetic pace of work, but also has been a model of his belief in spontaneity and creativity as a way of life.

Table 2

Some of the Themes and Concepts Which Moreno Emphasized in His Writings

1. Play as an element in culture and the helping relationship.

2. Catharsis—its place in history, drama, religion, and psychodrama.

3. The place of warm-up in everyday life—e.g., boxing, sexual activity, group process, psychotherapy.

4. Imagination—the creative potential; applications of fantasy.

5. Spontaneity and creativity as primary elements of human growth.

6. The importance of nonverbal communication, body tone and movement, posture, position, territoriality, lightning, sound, music, colors, textures, body contact, laughter, and humor as elements in human relationships.

7. The social network, family network, community and societal network, and *interpersonal transaction* (therapeutic milieu), and so forth.

8. Here-and-now,—an essentially existential approach.

9. Focus on *process* rather than *content*.

10. Acting-out (in the service of the ego) as an expression of act-hunger, can be a synthetic rather than dissociative phenomenon.

11. The religious implications and applications of subjective, creative and spontaneous man in relation to a creative Cosmos.

12. Utilization of wide variety of methods, techniques, and technologies to help the client explore the dimensions of his experience (rather than restriction to one technique), i.e., eclecticism.

13. The applications of role-reversal to child-rearing, the teaching of empathy and interpersonal sensitivity.

14. The use of therapy *in-situ,* (i.e. the intervention on-the-spot, exploring the problem in the context and social network from which it arose), now applied in milieu therapy, residential treatment centers for children and adolescents, and other contexts.

References

Bischof, Ledford J. *Interpreting personality theories*. New York: Harper & Row, 1964.

Bradford, L., Gibb, J.R., and Benne, K.D. *T-Group theory and laboratory method: Innovations in re-education*. New York: John Wiley, 1964. Classical work on one of the roots of "sensitivity training" movement.

Corsini, Raymond J. Historic background of group psychotherapy. *Group Psychotherapy,* 1955, *8*(3), 219-225.

Gazda, George (Ed.) *Innovations in group psychotherapy*. Springfield, Ill.: Charles C Thomas, 1968.

Jones, Maxwell. *The therapeutic community*. New York: Basic Books, 1953. Comments on use of psychodrama in therapeutic milieu.

Meiers, Joseph. Origins and development of group psychotherapy—Historical survey, 1930-1945. *Sociometry,* 1949, *8,* 499.

Moreno, J. L. *Who shall survive? Foundations of sociometry, group psychotherapy, and sociodrama*. Beacon, New York: Beacon House, 1953 (Revised). A classic text.

Moreno, J.L. *International handbook of group psychotherapy*. New York: Philosophical Library, 1966.

Moreno, J. L. Reflections on my method of group psychotherapy and psychodrama, in H. Greenwald (Ed.) *Active psychotherapy*. Chicago: Atherton, 1967.

Moreno, J. L. The Viennese origins of the encounter movement. *Group Psychotherapy,* 1969, *22*(3-4), 7-16.

Moreno, Zerka Toeman. The seminal mind of J. L. Moreno and his influence upon the present generation. *Group Psychotherapy,* 1967, *20*(3-4). 218-229.

Renouvier, P. The group psychotherapy movement and J. L. Moreno. *Group Psychotherapy,* 1955, *11*(1-2), 69-88.

Treadwell, Thomas and Treadwell, Jean. The pioneer of the group encounter movement. *Group Psychotherapy,* 1972, *25*(1-2), 16-26.

Weiner, Hannah. J. L. Moreno—Mr. Group Psychotherapy. *Group Psychotherapy,* 1968, *21*(3-4), 144-150.

Bibliography

This bibliography is designed to aid the reader in finding some of the most relevant materials currently available. In the interest of brevity, I have made some omissions for the following reasons: (1) many articles written before 1967 have been listed elsewhere by Corsini (1965-67), Haskell, and Siroka (1971); (2) I have included references of important articles from Moreno's journals which I consider essential, but I recommend the reader to complement this book with a study of their bibliographies; (3) the foreign psychiatric and psychological journals have many useful articles; the books by Ancelin-Schutzenberger, Leutz, Weil, and the *Bulletin de Psychologie* contain excellent bibliographies of the international literature.

Articles and books which are more related to specific subjects are noted in the section on references after each chapter in this book.

Ancelin-Schutzenberger, Anne. *Précis de psychodrama*. Paris: Editions Universitaires, 1970 (Revised ed.). Best text in French.

Blatner, Howard. Comments on commonly-held reservations about psychodrama. *Group Psychotherapy,* 1968, *21*(1), 20-25.

Blatner, Howard. Goal-orientation and action-orientation as two criteria for patient selection in group psychotherapy. *Voices,* 1968, *4*(3), 90-95.

Blatner, Howard. The place of psychodramatic methods in the armamentarium of the psychotherapist. Presentation at the ninth annual meeting of Western Division of American Psychiatric Association, Seattle, August 1969.

Blatner, Howard (Ed.) *Practical aspects of psychodrama*. Belmont, Calif.: Author, 1968. This was the first book, privately produced, which has been revised continuously to finally become the present book.

Blatner, Howard (Ed.) *Psychodrama, role-playing, and action methods. Theory and practice*. Thetford, England: Author, 1970. This mimeo graphed book was the second in the series. It is also out of print

Bulletin de psychologie, 1969-70, *23*(285, 13-16). Special edition of this journal with about 40 articles on psychodrama, in French. Edited by Université de Paris.

Burwell, D. M. Psychodrama. *Canadian Journal of Occupational Therapists,* Winter 1969, *36,* 141-144.

Carp, E. A. *Psychodrama.* Amsterdam: Scheltema and Holkema, 1949.

Corsini, Raymond J. Immediate therapy in groups, in George M. Gazda (Ed.) *Innovations to group psychotherapy.* Springfield, Ill.: Charles C Thomas, 1968.

Corsini, Raymond J. *Role-playing in psychotherapy.* Chicago: Aldine Press, 1967. One of the basics for any library on psychodrama. Has very good glossary and annotated bibliography. Has some approaches to groups which may not apply to all situations. Bibliography includes many items not in this bibliography.

Corsini, Raymond J., Shaw, M. E., and Blake, R. R. *Role-playing in business and industry.* New York: Free Press, 1961. Very good book, with fine annotated bibliography especially related to this field, and many articles not noted in this present bibliography.

Daly, Dennis C. Psychodrama as a core technique in milieu therapy. Unpublished doctoral dissertation, St. Louis University, 1961.

Fine, Leon and Matsumura, Kohei. Psychodrama in Japan: The nonverbal session. *Journal of Psychodrama, Group Psychotherapy, and Role-Playing,* (Tokyo) 1964, *1,* 23-63.

Fine, Reiko. Psychodance. *Group Psychotherapy,* 1962, *15*(3-4), 203.

Finney, Ben C. Say it again: an active therapy technique. *Psychotherapy: Theory, Research and Practice,* 1972, *9*(2), 157-165.

Greenberg, Ira A. *Psychodrama and audience attitude change.* Beverly Hills: Behavioral Studies Press, 1968.

Greewald, Harold (Ed.) *Active psychotherapy.* New York: Atherton Press, 1967. Many varied articles on methods which demand active intervention in therapy—recommended for any therapist who wishes to get good eclectic approach.

Greenwald, Harold, Play therapy for children over 21. *Psychotherapy: Theory, Research and Practice,* 1967, *4*(1), 44.

Haas, Robert Bartlett. *Psychodrama and sociodrama in American education.* Beacon, New York: Beacon House, 1949. One of the important books on psychodrama, consisting of many papers.

Haas, Robert Bartlett and Moreno, J. L. Psychodrama as a projective technique, in Harold H. Anderson and G. L. Anderson (Eds.) *An introduction to projective techniques*. Englewood Cliffs, N. J.: Prentice-Hall, 1961.

Haskell, Martin. The drug addict, role-playing, and group psychotherapy—the need for a new approach. *Group Psychotherapy,* 1958, *11*(3-4), 197-202.

Haskell, *The psychodramatic method*. Long Beach, Calif.: Role Training Associates, 1968. Short booklet which should be a part of any basic library on psychodrama. This booklet can be obtained from Role Training Associates. P. O. Box 15085. Long Beach, California, 90815.

Hollander, Carl. The social dynamics of therapeutic recreation. *Hospital and Community Psychiatry,* August 1967, 226-229.

Kahn, Samuel. *Psychodrama explained*. New York: Philosophical Library, 1964.

Kreitler, Hans and Eblinger, S. Individual psychotherapy, group psychotherapy, psychodrama, in Jules Masserman and J. L. Moreno (Eds.) *Reviews and integrations,* Volume 5 of *Progress in psychotherapy*. New York, Grune and Stratton, 1960.

Krojanker, Rolf. Some new techniques in psychodrama and hypodrama. *Archives de Criminologia, Neuro-Psiquiatria,* 1963, *11*, 411.

Lebovici, Serge, Psychoanalytic applications of psychodrama. *Journal of Social Therapy,* 1958, *2*, 280.

Lebovici, Serge, Psychoanalytical group psychotherapy. *Group Psychotherapy,* 1956, *9*(3-4), 282.

Lebovici, Serge. Uses of psychodrama in psychiatric diagnosis. *International Journal of Sociometry and Sociatry,* 1960, *3*, 175.

Lebovici, Serge, Diatkine, R. and Kestenberg, E. Applications of psychoanalysis to group psychotherapy and psychodrama therapy in France. *Group Psychotherapy,* 1952, *5*(1-2), 38.

Leutz, Greta A. Transference, empathy, and tele. *Group Psychotherapy and Psychodrama,* 1971, *24*(3-4), 107-112.

Leutz, Greta A. and Petzold, H. (Eds.) *Zeitschrift fur praktische psychologie,* December 1970, *5*(8). Special issue on psychodrama.

Levit, Grace and Jennings, Helen H. Learning through role-playing, in Warren G. Bennis, Kenneth D. Benne and Robert Chin (Eds.) *The planning of change*. New York: Holt, Rinehart & Winston, 1966.

Listwan, Ignacy A. Psychodrama. *Medical Journal of Australia,* 1955, *42*(15), 524-527.

Margolis, H. Psychodrama approach to diagnosis in casework. *Journal of Social Casework,* 1946, 27, 291.

Moreno, J. L. Actual trends in group psychotherapy. *Group Psychotherapy,* 1963, *16* (1-2), 117.

Moreno, J. L. The dilemma of existentialism, daseinanalyse and psychodrama. *International Journal of Sociometry and Sociatry,* 1955, *4*, 55-63.

Moreno, J. L. The discovery of the spontaneous man. *Group*

Psychotherapy, 1956, *8*(1-2), 103-219, 329-345.

Moreno, J. L. Fundamental rules and techniques of psychodrama, in Jules Masserman and J. L. Moreno (Eds.) *Techniques of psychotherapy*. Volume 3 of *Progress in psychotherapy*. New York: Grune and Stratton, 1958.

Moreno, J. L. (Ed.) *Group Psychotherapy*. The main journal of the current movement. Most of the articles related to psychodrama have been published in this journal. In 1971, the title was changed to *Group Psychotherapy and Psychodrama*.

Moreno, J. L. (Ed.) *International handbook of group psychotherapy*. New York: Philosophical Library, 1966.

Moreno, J. L. (Ed.) International Journal of Sociometry and Sociatry. 1956-1964, 1-5.

Moreno, J. L. Mental catharsis and psychodrama. *Sociometry,* 1940, *3*(1), 209.

Moreno, J. L. Psychiatry in the twentieth centry—the function of universalia: Time, space, reality, and the cosmos. *Group Psychotherapy*, 1967, *20*(1-2), 146.

Moreno, J. L. *Psychodrama*, Vol. 1. Beacon, New York: Beacon House, 1946 (Revised 1964). A classic and basic text.

Moreno, J.L., Psychodrama in Sylvano Arieti (Ed.) *American handbook of psychiatry*, Vol. 2. New York: Basic Books, 1959. One of the best brief reviews on the subject.

Moreno, J. L. Psychodrama, in W. Wolff (Ed.) *Contemporary psychotherapists examine themselves*. Springfield, Ill.: Charles C Thomas, 1956.

Moreno, J. L. *Psychodrama: Action therapy and principles of practice,* Vol. 3, Beacon, New York: Beacon House, 1969.

Moreno, J. L. Psychodrama and group psychotherapy. *Sociometry,* 1946, *9*(3-4), 249.

Moreno, J. L. Psychodrama of a pre-marital couple. *Sociatry* 1948, *2*(2), 103-120.

Moreno, J. L. A psychodramatic frustration test. *Group Psychotherapy,* 1954, *6*(3), 145-173.

Moreno, J. L. Psychodramatic production techniques. *Group Psychotherapy,* 1952, *4*(4), 243.

Moreno, J. L. Reflections on my method of group psychotherapy and psychodrama. *CIBA Symposium*, 1963, *11*(4), 148-157.

Moreno, J. L. Significance of the therapeutic format and the place of acting out in psychotherapy. *Group Psychotherapy,* 1955, *8*(3-4), 7-19.

Moreno, J.L. *Sociatry: a journal of group and intergroup therapy,* 1947-1948, 1-2. This journal then became *Group Psychotherapy*.

Moreno, J. L. (Ed.) *Sociometry, a journal of interpersonal relations,* 1937-1947, 1-10. It has continued since that time under the supervision of a board of directors who are involved purely with sociological issues.

Moreno, J. L. *Sociometry–Experimental method and the science of society* (Foreword by Gardner Murphy). Beacon, New York: Beacon House, 1953. (Revised ed.)

Moreno, J. L. *The sociometry reader*. New York: Free Press, 1960.

Moreno, J. L. Spontaneity, creativity, and human potentialities, in H. A. Otto (Ed.) *Explorations in human potentialities*. Springfield, Ill.: Charles C Thomas, 1966.

Moreno, J. L. Spontaneity training of children. *Sociometry*, 1938, *1*, 20-23. Psychodrama monograph #4.

Moreno, J. L. *Das stegreiftheater* (the Theater of Spontaneity). Beacon, New York: Beacon House, 1947.

Moreno, J. L. Therapeutic aspects of psychodrama. *Psychiatric opinion*, 1966, *3*(2), 36-4?

Moreno, J. L. *Who shall survive? Foundations of sociometry, group psychotherapy, and sociodrama*. Beacon, New York: Beacon House, 1953 (Revised ed.)

Moreno, J. L. *The words of the father*. Beacon, New York: Beacon House, 1941. (1971 Paperback re-issue.)

Moreno, J. L. and Moreno, Zerka T. Objective analysis of the group psychotherapy movement. *Group Psychotherapy*, 1960, *13*(3-4), 233.

Moreno, J. L. and Moreno, Zerka T. *Psychodrama*, Vol. 2. Beacon, New York: Beacon House, 1956.

Moreno, Zerka T. Psychodrama in a well baby clinic. *Group Psychotherapy*, 1951, *4*(1-2), 100-106.

Moreno, Zerka T. Psychodramatic rules, techniques, and adjunctive methods. *Group Psychotherapy*, 1965, *18*(1-2), 73-86.

Moreno, Zerka T. A survey of psychodramatic techniques. *ACTA Psychotherapeutica*, 1959, *7*, 197-206.

Naruse, Gosaku. Recent development of psychodrama and hypnodrama in Japan. *Group Psychotherapy*, 1959, *12*(3-4), 258-261.

O'Connell Walter. Psychothcrapy for everyman—A look at action therapy. *Journal of Existentialism*, Fall 1966, *7*, 85.

O'Connell, Walter and Hanson, P. Patient's cognitive changes in human relations training. *Journal of Individual Psychology*, May 1970, *26*, 57-63.

Ohlsen, Merle M. *Group counseling*. New York: Holt, Rinehart & Winston, 1969. Fair chapter on role-playing.

Parrish, Marguerite. The effect of short term psychodrama on chronic schizophrenic patients. *Group Psychotherapy*, 1959, *12*(1-2), 15-26.

Parrish, Marguerite. Psychodrama, description of application and reviews of technique. *Group Psychotherapy*, 1953, *6*(1-2), 74-77.

Pesso, Albert. *Experience in action*. New York University Press, 1972.

Seabourne, Barbara. The role of the auxiliary. Unpublished manuscript, St. Louis State Hospital, 1966.

Seabourne, Barbara. Role training. Unpublished manuscript, St. Louis

State Hospital, 1966.

Seabourne, Barbara. Rough notes on differences between group psychotherapy and individual therapy. Unpublished manuscript, St Louis State Hospital, 1966.

Seabourne, Barbara. So you want to start a group. Unpublished manuscript, St. Louis State Hospital, 1966.

Seabourne, Barbara. Some hints on dealing with various kinds of protagonists. Unpublished manuscript, St. Louis State Hospital, 1966.

Seabourne, Barbara. Warm-up of protagonist and auxiliaries. Unpublished manuscript, St. Louis State Hospital, 1966.

Shoobs, Nahum E. Individual psychology and psychodrama. *Journal of Individual Psychology,* 1956, *12*(1), 280-289.

Simos, Jack. The use of drama in group work. Unpublished masters thesis, University of Minnesota, 1950.

Siroka, Robert W., Siroka, Ellen and Schloss, Gilbert (Eds.) *Sensitivity training and group encounter—an introduction.* New York: Grosset and Dunlap, 1971. One of the really outstanding anthologies—with noted authors writing on the history of groups; relationships to psychodrama are included. Excellent bibliography.

Sturm, Israel Eli. Implications of role-playing methodology for clinical procedure. *Behavior Therapy,* 1971, *2,* 88-96.

Theiner, Eric C. An approach to the manpower problem: Psychodrama as conducted in a military setting. *American Psychologist,* 1969, *24*(7), 686-687.

Thorne, Brian. Psychodramatic techniques in counseling. *The Counsellor,* December 1971. Journal of National Association of Educational Counsellors, Great Britain.

Uhl, Anita. The psychodrama—a new technique in psychotherapy. Unpublished masters thesis, Stanford University, 1942.

Weil, Pierre. *Psicodrama.* Rio de Janeiro: Edicons Cepa, 1967. Text in Portuguese.

Weiner, Hannah. The identity of the psychodramatist and the underground of psychodrama. *Group Psychotherapy,* 1967, *20*(3-4), 114-117.

Weiner, Hannah. Psychodrama and television programming. *International Journal of Sociometry and Sociatry,* 1966, *5*(1-2), 11.

Yablonsky, Lewis and Enneis, James. Psychodrama, theory and practice, in Frieda Fromm-Reichmann and J. L. Moreno (Eds.) *Progress in psychotherapy,* Vol. 1. New York: Grune and Stratton, 1956.

Index